LEAN CULTURE

COLLECTED PRACTICES AND CASES

PRODUCTIVITY PRESS

New York, New York

Most Productivity Press books are available at quantity discounts when purchased in bulk. For more information contact our Customer Service Department (888-319-5852). Address all other inquiries to:

Productivity Press
444 Park Avenue South, 7th floor
New York, NY 10016
United States of America
Telephone: 212-686-5900
Fax: 212-686-5411
E-mail: info@productivitypress.com

Material originally appeared in the *Lean Manufacturing Advisor*, 1999-2005.

Library of Congress Cataloging-in-Publication Data
Lean culture : collected practices & cases.
    p. cm.
 Includes index.
 ISBN 1-56327-326-8 (alk. paper)
 1. Organizational effectiveness. 2. Organizational change. 3. Corporate culture. I. Productivity Press.
 HD58.9.L42 2005
 658.3'1–dc22

                                                          2005010827

08 07 06 05 9 8 7 6 5 4 3 2 1

Contents

Part II: Staff Development 55

Part III: Sustaining Change 101

Introduction

The hard part of implementing a lean transformation, according to most experts, is dealing with the "soft" issues – meaning culture change.

Applying 5S to a work area, conducting a kaizen event, creating a value stream map – these are all relatively easy and can be accomplished in a fairly short period of time once those involved have gone through some basic training in the concepts. The real challenge comes in building and sustaining a lean culture – in getting your workers to live and breathe lean, actively supporting and buying into lean concepts and philosophy, always searching for ways to eliminate waste, improving processes and providing greater value for your customers.

For your transformation to be successful, lean must become the way you do business on a daily basis – and the way your employees believe you should do business on a daily basis.

Because the "soft" issues are so important, *Lean Manufacturing Advisor* — a newsletter that each month chronicles how companies are implementing lean production[1] — has regularly offered articles addressing these issues. This compilation of these articles includes both case studies of how cultural strategies are imple-

---

[1] For more information regarding the articles in this book, including the original dates of publication, please refer to the citations section.

mented and advice from leading experts about the key success factors in culture change.

The book is divided into three sections. The first of these addresses ways to get started – how you educate workers, build support and buy-in, and gain momentum for lean initiatives. Since lean implementations require people who know how to make them happen, the second section focuses on staff development – how to select, train and even compensate lean leaders for your transformation. And because so many attempted transformations stumble and stall, the third section tackles the challenges of sustaining change.

The library of lean literature accumulated over the years includes relatively few books dedicated to the topic of culture change, and even fewer that offer a range of case studies. We hope this publication will be a meaningful and practical addition to your lean bookshelf.

Ralph Bernstein
Editor
Lean Manufacturing Advisor

Part I
Building Support

OVERVIEW

Sometimes the most perplexing challenge facing a company embarking on a lean transformation is how to get started. Sometimes it is the question of how to expand an initial effort to get everyone in the company on board. The chapters in this section help address both of these issues.

We begin with a case study of Hartz Mountain, where strong top management support for lean was already in place. That support came from new management as they assumed leadership of a company with no history of lean. This chapter chronicles how an aggressive management style helped achieve rapid improvement while also transforming company culture.

While perhaps not as aggressive as the leaders at Hartz, top managers at Jabil Circuit were also determined to transform their entire enterprise. Their approach – training, new incentives, changes in processes – is outlined in Chapter 2.

Executives at Tigerpoly regarded culture change as being so critical to their plans for a lean transformation that they made cultural issues their top priority. Chapter 3 describes their efforts to strengthen the level of expertise among managers, provide training to the workforce and begin their transformation cautiously, with a pilot project.

One often-overlooked aspect of enabling culture change is the role of the human resources department, both from a support and management perspective, and in regard to training. Chapter 4 explains how the HR department at Aeroquip Inoac has contributed to the transformation of that company's culture.

Employees will only buy into lean culture change if they believe that they are a part of the culture, and that their opinion matters.

One way to build that belief is to have an active suggestion program, in which not only are employees encouraged to offer ideas, but the company takes those suggestions seriously and acts on them. The Sensormatic plant in Puerto Rico has developed such a program, described in Chapter 5.

Building buy-in can be especially challenging when the workforce is unionized, particularly when the union and management have not been on the best of terms. Chapter 6 discusses how union workers and managers at the Lukens steel plant overcame their animosity to transform operations and build a new culture.

Sometimes lean initiatives lack top management support. For those middle managers trying to convince higher-ups of the value of lean, Chapter 7 offers some words of wisdom from Art Byrne on how you can sell lean to your CEO. As the former CEO of Wiremold, Byrne speaks with authority.

Sunstar Butler is one of those companies that began lean without top management backing. Chapter 8 explains how a few managers there launched what was almost a surreptitious campaign to win over its leaders, using the success of early efforts to make the case for an enterprise-wide transformation.

Which strategies and tactics work best for you will depend on your particular situation. But the range of approaches described in these tales will almost certainly give you some ideas for building support within your own company.

1

Aggressive Management Builds a New Hartz Mountain Culture

July, 2003

Dr. Al Gunneson, corporate vice president for strategic advancement at The Hartz Mountain Corporation, describes plant manager Bill Judge as a malcontent.

That's a compliment.

In fact, it's one of the reasons Judge holds his current job, managing the nearly 400 employees at the company's main manufacturing site in Bloomfield, N.J. Following a leveraged buyout in 2000, and a decision to aggressively transform Hartz using lean manufacturing principles, "we wanted to promote from within,"

Vice President Dr. Al Gunneson, Hartz Mountain

Gunneson recalls. "We took people who were aggressive and somewhat malcontents, frustrated with the way we do business, even if they haven't done the job before. We take bright people and put them in over their head, with the understanding that they can come to us for mentoring and it won't be taken as a sign of weakness."

Gunneson likes to shake things up. Since joining Hartz in 2001 to help lead its transformation, six out of eight vice presidents have left the company, reductions in inventory were achieved within a short time by rapidly closing warehouses, production lines have been redesigned and raw material supermarkets created to feed production.

Plant Manager Bill Judge

The efforts are already producing benefits for Hartz. For example, inventory was valued at about $70 million at the time of the buyout; the number has since dropped to somewhere in the mid-$40 million range, and executives hope to bring it down to around $33 million by the end of this year. That's just one of a range of improvements achieved so far (see sidebar, page 6).

In addition to the financial benefits, Hartz is already well into a transformation of its corporate culture. From the corner offices to the shop floor, a striking enthusiasm is evident among employees. Production managers talk about their jobs with smiles as they describe improvements that have been made.

Such a change does not come from just one person. In addition to working closely with Hartz President Robert Devine, Gunneson is joined in his efforts by Judge, a 10-year company veteran promoted to manage Bloomfield, and Bill Martin, a 27-year veteran who was promoted from vice president to chief operations officer. They seem to share Gunneson's passion for the business and his energy for the job. Moreover, they follow his lead in pursuing an aggressive, hands-on management style while simultaneously seeking to empower employees and encourage their efforts.

It's all part of a very deliberate, detailed strategy to take a traditional manufacturing company facing a variety of problems and "make the elephant dance," as Martin said when he and Gunneson spoke at the 2003 Logistics Forum, a conference sponsored by Richmond Events. Their efforts to create a new sense of urgency at Hartz — which include working with several different

Hartz now stores raw material in supermarkets near production lines like this one at its Bloomfield, NJ plant.

consultants — arc based on specific, clearly stated goals and objectives (see sidebar, page 8). And at the forefront of those efforts is an aggressive push for change through a direct management style designed to quickly convert employees to the new culture, eagerly welcoming those who join in — and pushing aside those who don't.

A Fearless Blitz

Hartz, whose headquarters are in Secaucus, N.J., is a name well-known among pet owners. The almost $400 million company's products range from food for birds, fish and small animals, to flea and tick solutions, to toys for pets.

The family of founder Max Stern operated the company for more than 75 years, but then spun it off to an investment group including members of Hartz management in December, 2000. (The Stern family still operates a real estate company under the Hartz Mountain Industries name.)

Substance Along With Style

Some of the accomplishments at Hartz since the lean transformation was launched a little over two years ago include:

- The value of inventory has declined by nearly $30 million. Inventory turns have increased from around 8 or 9 to as high as 35, in some categories.
- SG&A (selling, general and administrative) expenses went down last year by about 12 percent.
- Efficiency, measured in pieces per man hour, went up from 75 percent to 98 percent.
- Changeover times have been reduced significantly — typically from a few hours to a few minutes.
- Approximately 56,000 square feet of floor space have been freed up, enabling Hartz to transfer some operations from other locations to Bloomfield. More space improvements are coming; for example, the company is in the process of consolidating six separate maintenance shops within the Bloomfield site into one.
- Shipments of products to Wal-Mart now go directly from the Bloomfield plant, rather than going first to another Hartz location in Jersey City, N.J. for further processing, saving $350,000.
- More than 85 percent of all shipments are now full trailer loads, rather than LTL, or less than trailer load. LTLs used to make up the majority of shipments. The change has yielded significant cost savings.
- Overtime is down from about 8,800 hours per month to 800 per month, equivalent to a 220-person reduction.
- Service levels improved from around 86 percent to better than 98 percent.

Without the Stern family's support and with a new debt load, operating fundamentally more efficiently suddenly became a top priority for newly-independent Hartz. Gunneson originally was brought in as a consultant to help launch the lean transformation. However, since Judge had never been a plant manager before, and since COO Martin, who previously worked in areas such as finance and distribution, was becoming involved in manufacturing for the first time in his career, Devine wanted additional executive-

Redesigned production lines at the Hartz Bloomfield plant take up significantly less floor space.

level expertise in manufacturing and asked Gunneson to join the company full-time.

"When the place is on fire, you've got to come in and hit it with an extinguisher," Gunneson declared during a recent plant tour. "We had to blitz the company, to put out fires and recover 'quick hit' cash fast. Then we focused on the new culture, which allowed concurrent streamlining and re-engineering to be effective and lasting."

A key principle of the new culture is making "radical change without fear of failure," he adds. "I told people I want big, bold mistakes. They looked at me like I had two heads. But it's because I want big successes. On the ones that don't work, fail fast and get on to the big winners."

Voices From the Floor

One example of how the culture change is permeating the company is Larry Cortale, a production manager, who Gunneson says used to be "always in our face" as well as "unhappy" and "cantankerous. So we promoted him."

"The way we were going, I didn't think we'd survive," Cortale says. But today, "to me, it's like running my own little company. We decide what we're going to make. I find it exciting. It's a challenge

Lean and Agile, Plus SOMO

One of the stated goals of the Hartz transformation is to create what the company calls a Lean and Agile enterprise. Lean is defined as "a tactical, bottom up effort to drive all waste out of the supply chain," while Agile is defined as "a strategic, top down effort to create fast, flexible supply chains to enable mass customization capability."

COO Bill Martin describes an operational goal: "To make every single product every single week, and to be able to make any product any day."

Another key part of the transformation is the adoption of a strategy called SOMO — sell one, make one. This system involves calculation of average weekly sales based on the last four weeks of activity. That average is used to drive production. All the sales people have to do is make sure production is aware when there's going to be a change, such as a special promotion. All the data feeds into the MRP system.

In a related action, Hartz has stopped using its forecasting system. However, the company still makes extensive use of information technology — for example, just-launched software is looking at retail point-of-sale data (provided by some customers) and incoming orders three times a day to flag exceptions directly to planners.

Cross-functional category business teams have been formed. Processes are mapped. Kaizen events take place about every two weeks. Several production lines have been converted to U-shaped cells, and more are being changed. Raw materials are now located in internal supermarkets near production lines.

The company is working closely with suppliers, who are often involved in kaizen events. Use of VMI (vendor-managed inventory) has increased to the point where it now accounts for 50 percent of sales by volume.

every day. It's fun." At several points, he and Judge ended up telling the same stories, describing a change that was made, or an amusing conversation. Before the change, Cortale says, "you were like a robot. You would just do what you had to do."

Sylvester Jackson, a production supervisor and a 30-year company veteran, is equally enthusiastic. "People listen to you," he beams.

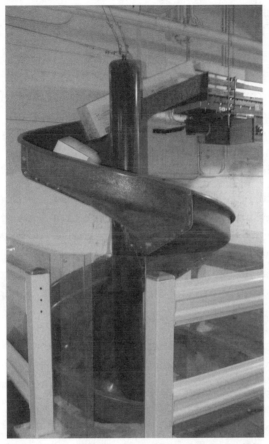

Hartz workers created a spiral slide so products could be moved quickly from one floor to another without damage.

"It's been great. I'm having a beautiful time. You can see it on the floor, everybody pitching in. It's terrific."

Jack Sakalsky, a senior manager, boasts that "everybody works together. Everybody knows we have to keep the company as profitable as possible. I'm real optimistic about the future."

Butting Heads

That's not to say everyone jumped on board right away. Initially, there was plenty of resistance from the old culture. For example, Gunneson recalled the fact that the company was buying containers from a supplier in Florida whose minimum order was 40,000 — far more than the company needed in the short term. He questioned a Hartz purchasing agent about it; Gunneson, in a whiny impression of the agent's voice, recalls him saying, "Well, Al, you have to understand, the supplier has these logistics issues..."

"Not my problem," was Gunneson's brusque reply.

In another example, managers were moving slowly — too slowly, in Gunneson's view — to reduce inventory in the plant. So Gunneson, who preaches that "inventory is evil," decided to close a 33,000-square-foot warehouse the company also used, and to do so within three months. "That forced us to reorganize the plant — and fast," he states.

Judge, the plant manager, shares some of Gunneson's management style. He strides quickly through the plant (which makes 69 percent of all Hartz products), greeting employees by name everywhere he goes, picking up any bits of trash he spots. His words come out in a rapid-fire pace as he describes how this line was changed, that internal supermarket was created, this space was cleared.

Judge notes that he had to put old ways of thinking behind him, such as his desire to make sure a label room contained three days worth of every label the company uses. (Now many shelves in the room are empty; "when we need shelves, we come here," Judge says, smiling.) He adds that he used to be a person who spent a lot of time reviewing information. "I was the analyzer," he comments.

"And I was the cliff-jumper," Gunneson interjects.

Hartz is making rapid progress, and Gunneson foresees a time when improved results will enable the company to make acquisitions.

Getting to that point depends in large part, he believes, on converting to a lean culture where employees are encouraged to promote change and given the authority to make it.

"We understand that any engineer can shrink the process," he said at the Logistics Forum presentation. "But you can't dump it into a workforce that can't do it because management won't let them.

"When the perception is achieved that doing it differently is better for me and the company — voila, you've changed the culture."

TAKEAWAYS

- A management push for change must be supported by clear goals and objectives.
- A central concept is that not every new idea must succeed, so there is no fear of failure.
- One approach to production is SOMO — sell one, make one.

2

The Ways to Win Hearts and Minds

July, 2002

How do you turn your employees and managers into enthusiastic supporters of a lean transformation?

The question is important because employee buy-in is critical to the success of a lean implementation. Unless you capture your employees' hearts and minds as you change how they work, improvement at your company will be anything but continuous.

Jabil Circuit, which designs and assembles circuit boards and provides other electronic manufacturing services – is just a few years into a lean journey, but has already achieved significant gains. And company executives are quick to emphasize that employee involvement has been a key part of that success.

"Previously, it was a management-type operation," explains Dave Couch, senior director of operations. "Now, we want you to take control of the line. We want you to stop the line as soon as you see an issue. People on the floor have ownership. It really changed the perception of who they were and what authority they had.

"Jabil's culture today is very important to us. There's a can-do attitude to getting things done. It's a little bit different than the way we've done things in the past."

The company's lean initiatives got under way in 1998, and the benefits so far include:

- An 85 percent improvement in productivity, measured as boards per person per hour.

- A reduction of the floor space required for production, in some cases by almost 60 percent.

- An 85 percent reduction in defects per million pieces.

- A "10x" reduction of scrap.

Couch comments: "The beauty is, you go on the floor, and people are just gushing with the opportunity to come to work, and know they have a team of five or eight or ten people they work with, and they have ownership of a part of Jabil. They really leave work knowing that 'I did something good today.' The gains are pretty huge. Now we have people really involved in the business. We weren't bad before, but we're a whole lot better when we got to the other side."

A Need to Keep Up

In Jabil's case, lean manufacturing was not something driven by a sudden epiphany of top management. Rather, the company found that most of its customers in the automotive industry (which accounts for about 6 percent of Jabil's business, according to Couch) were pursuing lean initiatives – and expected Jabil to do the same.

So the company began a lean journey at its facility in Auburn Hills, Mich. That plant, a key source of products and services for automotive customers, is today the site furthest along in going lean, though other plants have launched similar initiatives, Couch notes.

Jabil is headquartered in St. Petersburg, Fla., and has more than 20 plants worldwide with annual sales in the neighborhood of $4 billion.

With roughly half its sales to the telecommunications industry, and another third in computers and computer peripherals, times have been tough for Jabil. For the second quarter of fiscal 2002, ending Feb. 28, 2002, Jabil reported a drop in revenue to $822 million, from $1.2 billion for the same period a year earlier. Net income was $15.3 million, down from $41.8 million.

However, the company said in a statement that "focusing on operational execution enabled it to post results for the quarter that were ahead of current Wall Street consensus expectations and in line with the expectations set forth by the company in December 2001." During the second quarter, the company improved inventory turns to nine and reduced the sales cycle by eight days.

Motivation and Training

The first part of Jabil's plan to become lean, Couch says, was "to get the buy-in of people who were going to be owners. We spent probably six months walking through what lean manufacturing meant to us, what that would look like. We broke it down to beliefs and paradigms. It was really to get people acquainted with it, get them prepared for change. The intent was that the folks on the shop floor would ultimately become owners of the process."

The first actual initiative at Jabil was the same first step taken by many companies launching a lean journey: 5S.

The methodology of 5S – sort, set in order, shine, standardize and sustain – is used to create a workplace that will meet the criteria of visual control and lean production.

"Probably the easiest to implement and the most beneficial is a strong 5S program," Couch says. "If we look at a lot of downtime issues and minor stoppages, a lot of that is related to organization of work space. We've seen a pretty significant improvement, not only in the appearance of the floor, but also in execution. If we maintain the floor at all times, we know where everything is at, and it makes it much cleaner, from an operations standpoint."

But Couch says 5S also has been a significant part of moving Jabil along its lean path. He credits 5S not only for making work areas cleaner and more efficient, but also for helping turn employees into lean champions.

Training has also been an important part of the lean effort. Couch notes that all employees are trained in multiple skills, the ability to handle multiple tasks, and interpersonal training – how to work as a team.

Incentives were changed as well. Couch says Jabil now operates on a "pay-for-skill" basis, meaning an employee is paid more for each additional skill he or she has mastered. "We wanted to have generalists. We wanted people to be as multi-skilled as possible," he says. "The only way to get people to warm up to that is, you give them incentive pay for each of the skills that you acquire."

An important part of achieving change, Couch stresses, was to let people know that they didn't have to be right every time.

He comments: "Our approach to implementation was that we really didn't know what was going to be successful and what wasn't going to work. We thought through what seemed to be the best pathways. If we went in a direction and it turned out to be wrong, we went back and fixed that. We physically changed the arrangement of machinery. We made a lot of mistakes, but we corrected them on a daily basis. We went out and changed something; if it wasn't the right thing to do, eight hours later in the shift change, we changed it again. People knew we were committed to the execution, and they saw it was OK to try something, even if it didn't work."

Different Ways to Work

Of course, along with incentives and training, many processes at Jabil have changed. For example, the company has moved to a kanban replenishment system with some suppliers, using software from i2 Corporation.

Mistake-proofing was useful when a new product was launched in mid-1999 – and its production was generating thousands of dollars of scrap each month.

The problem was traced to boards being oriented the wrong way before entering a robotic lamp insertion cell. While engineers began exploring costly photoelectric eyes and pneumatic cylinders as solutions, a workcell team member came up with a different idea – that cost only five cents.

Each board had a connector on only one side. The screw was tapped into the frame of the robotic cell in a horizontal position – which meant that a board that was reversed would bump against the connector and could not enter the workcell on the entrance conveyor. A team member could then change the orientation, eliminating the opportunity for scrap.

Now in 2002, Couch maintains, there is optimism and enthusiasm among Jabil workers because of the way they have been involved in the transformation.

"We view lean as a holistic business model. All parts of the organization must participate for it to be successful. You can't have just part and achieve benefits," Couch contends. "Commitment, tenacity and diligence are most important in execution."

He constantly returns to his themes of employee involvement and culture change.

He comments, "No one should go to me and say, 'why are we doing this?' They should have an understanding. They may not like what's being done, but as long as they understand what the goal is and know we're committed to success, they feel comfortable with that."

TAKEAWAYS

- At the start of a transformation, acquainting people with lean beliefs and paradigms builds buy-in.
- 5S is a good place to start, as a team-building exercise.
- Incentives must be aligned with objectives.

Creating a New Culture
Is Company's First Priority

May, 2003

Culture change is the tough part of a lean transformation; that's been repeated so many times it's almost a cliché.

But the corollary to that statement, which perhaps is not repeated quite as often, is that when you do a good job on culture change, you improve your chances for success.

That's what seems to have happened at Tigerpoly Manufacturing, a Grove City, Ohio, maker of molded and extruded plastic and rubber automotive parts, ranging from manifold covers to air induction parts.

As of May 2003, the company is less than two years into its lean journey, so it may be too soon to declare the effort a success. However, early results are good and momentum appears to be strong, which those involved attribute to the training and involvement of many employees.

"We've actually been very successful in disseminating lean culture," says Mark Bobulski, production manager. "We've been very successful in disseminating the feelings to a good number of individuals, more at the floor level."

"They've taken to heart what we all say, that the culture change is the hardest part," says Richard Niedermeier, senior management consultant with Productivity, Inc. "They put the most effort on getting that part of it done. They've got it into a position where it looks like it will sustain itself faster than most other companies. He doesn't have to go back and keep pushing the issue. They've gotten to the point that a majority of people involved so far understand this is a singular direction, and don't accept the possibility of going backwards."

Niedermeier became familiar with Tigerpoly's operations while teaching Productivity's Lean Manager Certificate Program (L-MAC). Bobulski was a student in the first session of that program, held in early 2002.

His enrollment in that program was a key step though not the only step in Tigerpoly's lean implementation, which stemmed from a top management decision in late 2001 to make operations more efficient and less costly by pursuing lean principles.

The leaders of the company had some knowledge of and expertise in lean, but that expertise was also needed at lower levels of management. Bobulski attended L-MAC to obtain the knowledge and skills. And about the same time, the company hired a lean manufacturing coordinator with experience at Toyota, Al Riza Yoneil.

A Pilot and Beyond

Bobulski began Tigerpoly's lean journey with a pilot project. It involved eliminating an assembly line – by changing a molding operation into a combined molding-and-assembly operation. "It was a small enough pilot that it could be easily managed by us, but at the same time was very visible. People saw what was going on. It was fairly critical for us to have something people could relate to," Bobulski notes.

Niedermeier agrees that the pilot project "was just the right scope. It was discrete manufacturing with both fabrication and assembly. The targets he set for himself were very conservative, in terms of lead time, waste and inventory. By the time he finished the four weeks, it had exceeded my expectations as to what I thought was there, in terms of what actually happened."

The pilot has already expanded to deployment of lean practices on two of Tigerpoly's five major product lines. "We're fine-tuning cells to the point where we had substantial work-in-process reductions – 1600 down to 30," Bobulski notes. "We've had part-path distances cut 40 to 50 percent easily, floor space reduction in the two deployed cells – a 45 percent reduction in space. Our value-added ratio is up by 90 percent, though it's still amazingly low. Still, it's a 90 percent change."

The first project after the pilot occurred last summer. Another followed beginning in October. The fall project, like the others, produced significant results.

Tigerpoly is gradually making use of the whole spectrum of lean tools and techniques.

"5S took about six months to get through the whole plant, mainly the first three S's (sort, set in order and shine). We're still fine-tuning the fourth and fifth S (standardize and sustain). That ties in very nicely with visual management. People on the floor are becoming more key – they're offering suggestions on how to improve visual management," Bobulski explains.

He also notes that work has begun on establishing a kanban system between supply sources and production cells. Value stream mapping has also been part of the process, and in one case the company will attempt kaikaku – a complete redesign of a process. Additionally, mistake-proofing efforts are also planned.

Building a Culture

But underlying it all has been the training and involvement of company workers, under what is called the Tigerpoly Lean Culture Initiative.

Training in 5S came first, and associates from all three shifts were paid overtime to attend training on Saturdays – a total of about

1,500 man-hours of training. They were given classroom instruction and shown training tapes. Everything was done in-house.

From there, the training expanded on to the shop floor. Associates went to their work areas to diagram operations, change layouts to improve efficiency, and clean, paint and straighten. The goal, Bobulski says, was to give them ownership of the process and the improvements.

Visual management systems came next, as part of the 5S implementation. Teams performed self-audits with 5S checklists.

As improvements have reduced manpower requirements, people have been reassigned and reallocated. No one has been laid off, though some reduction has occurred through attrition. A dedicated position of facilitator for lean manufacturing has been added, and an area in the plant has been dedicated to serve as a kind of think tank or war room. "People visit on a regular basis and jot down ideas," Bobulski notes.

He says his biggest surprise has been "that things are happening as fast as they are. Momentum is really starting to build here."

Despite the rapid pace, in a report he wrote describing lessons learned so far from the initiatives, Bobulski said it is important to "preach patience. In some environments it may take years to get results. Never promise openly for the six-month period, while building your base. Things should begin to turn around between the 8th to 12th month of initial operations, if you are doing things right."

Some of his other comments in the report were:

- "Take lean manufacturing as a leadership building process among line supervisors and operators. A new breed of leaders emerge through the projects."

- "Last but not the least is the networking. Always communicate and exchange ideas with your 'like-ones.' Remember lean management is still an evolving art and discipline, and you need all the outside support you can get to realize a lean organization."

Niedermeier observes that when managers gain lean expertise and begin implementations, they "realize that it's not a part-time job anymore – that they're going to have to think about how to do lean full-time."

TAKEAWAYS

- Making culture change a top priority may be the most effective way to achieve process change.
- An initial pilot project should be small enough to manage, but big enough to be highly visible.
- Training and visual systems are necessary to support culture change.

4

Tips for Molding a Kaizen Culture

February, 2000

As you know, the effort to implement TPM and lean won't sustain itself. You have to find ways to support the new practices or risk having people backslide into old habits at the first whiff of a problem or under the pressures that invariably build at the end of the month or quarter.

We've written about how a continuous improvement office helps to sustain the transformation. ("How to Create And Staff a JIT Promotion Office," February, 1998.) But there are other measures you can take so company culture supports the revolution and encourages people's buy-in.

One organization that has done a lot of culture-building is the Aeroquip Inoac Company plant in Fremont, Ohio. It has explicitly concentrated on developing a continuous improvement culture since the company was formed by an American-Japanese joint venture in 1989. The combined human resources/training department there plays an active role in supporting this kaizen culture, a challenge that too few HR organizations have taken up.

We talked to Dorothy Camrata, HR administrator, Kim Jones, facilitator/trainer, and Sue Cheek, facilitator/trainer about some of the key elements of the plant's supporting culture that involve the combined HR/training department. These elements fall into four

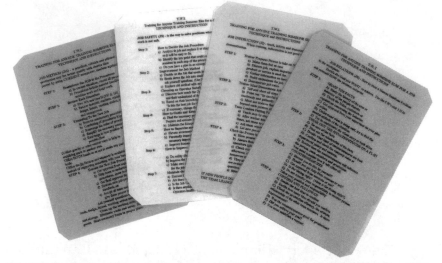

Help Is in the Cards – After supervisors complete the four-part Training Within Industry (TWI) course, they receive these four 3 x 5-inch cards, one for each subject covered in the course. The handy pocket-sized cards have step-by-step guidelines for how supervisors can assist hourly employees in four key areas: Job Instructions, Job Methods, Job Relations, and Job Safety. "They're very simply made," said Sue Cheek, facilitator/trainer. "We just print them on a color copier and laminate them ourselves."

main categories: small group activity; support activity, education activity, and management activity.

1. Small Group Activity

The continuous improvement culture began to form during the first year of the joint venture. Inoac Corporation contributed the kaizen philosophy with its emphasis on identifying and eliminating waste and Aeroquip supplied the factory, workforce, and the bulk of the management.

Americans sent to Japan for training returned with an appreciation for continuous improvement, said Camrata. A wave of plant closings in the northwest Ohio region also had made employees receptive to the concept of continuous improvement as a way of saving jobs. The importance of adopting a kaizen philosophy was promoted early on by Operations Vice President Mike Beebe, which helped the new culture take root. "If it's important to upper management, it becomes important to the people," said Cheek.

The training in Japan introduced Americans to the practice of small groups holding daily pre-production meetings devoted to improving safety, quality, productivity, 5S housekeeping, and costs. They brought the idea back to Fremont. The meeting is used by team leaders to build enthusiasm, morale, and consciousness about improving safety, quality, costs and other key concepts about TPM and lean.

It also is used to educate. The plant sends team leaders three or four "continuous improvement handouts" each week. These one-page flyers educate leaders in an improvement tool or skill, such as the use of check sheets or tips for interpersonal skills.

The plant draws a direct correlation between the introduction of the preproduction meetings and the beginning of sharp declines in rework and scrap costs. These brief meetings, which began in 1991, were the first step in developing an array of small group activities.

"One of the things that really helped us to advance quickly was we didn't wait until all the bugs were worked out before we tried something," said Cheek. "We worked things out as we went. I think that really helped us to speed things along in small group activities."

As the following list illustrates, the Fremont plant uses a lot of teams to involve people in decision making and show an appreciation for their ideas. The net effect is an increase in people's self-esteem, which the company believes is the basis of continuous improvement. Fremont team activities include:

Quality Control (QC) Circles: Yes, they still exist in the U.S. QC circles have three to five members compared to five-to-ten members on the other teams. These are the basis of the plant's kaizen activities and are encouraged in all areas. Meeting once or twice a week for 15 minutes, circles can finish two or three projects annually. The company believes holding the preproduction meetings made introduction of QC circles easier. They are formed to attack such issues as quality problems, cost reduction, energy and materials savings, safety, ergonomics, or other issues that align with company goals and are within the group's area. The circles follow an 11-step discipline:

1. Form the group and pick a leader.

2. Pick a permanent name and logo.

3. Identify problems according to the "seven wastes" and related criteria.

4. Select a specific problem by asking a series of established questions.

5. Plan the action steps and timetable with a Gantt chart.

6. Investigate the current condition using the seven QC tools.

7. Establish specific values for the goal, such as cutting defects by 50 percent.

8. Analyze possible causes according to the 4Ms (manpower, machines, methods, and materials) and implement countermeasures.

9. Confirm the results of the countermeasures or return to the analysis in Step 8.

10. Standardize the effective countermeasure by revising standard work (with engineering's involvement), establishing visual controls and poka-yoke (mistake-proofing measures) and creating a control chart.

11. Prepare a summary sheet and savings estimate to receive recognition and rewards.

"People misunderstand QC circle activities and small group activities," said Cheek. "They think these groups are made to just go out and solve problems. Well, that's partly true. But another thing they do is study processes and how to avoid making mistakes."

Action Teams are launched by supervisors when a key measurement, such as defects, begins to go out of control. The team consists of the area team leader, operators, and often an engineer. They collect data and work on the problem until the source is corrected.

Cost Reduction Teams are similar to action teams but focus on habitual, long-term costly problems. Members come from management, engineering, supervision, and may include an operator.

Improvement Teams tackle big improvements in layout, equipment, or production materials. Membership on the team reflects the type of problem being addressed.

TPM Teams consist of operators, maintenance technicians, and supervisors or team leaders. They brainstorm activities for inclusion in preventive and productive maintenance efforts and TPM check sheets. Teams also clean machines, a hands-on exercise that serves as an inspection to identify and correct problems. The cross-functional composition and hands-on activities create a sense of equipment ownership among team members. The cross-functional makeup encourages people to share knowledge and educate each other. The TPM team also teaches new operators.

Danger Prediction Teams are small group activities formed when a new product is launched, an accident occurs, new equipment is introduced, or an annual worksite review is required. Team members are trained in problem solving and how to identify potentially dangerous conditions. They identify unsafe conditions, suggest countermeasures, and implement them in their areas. Conditions requiring maintenance or purchased items go through management. The teams stay with a project until completion at which time they file a report with the Safety Department.

A standardized set of forms and procedures is the glue that holds together this variety of team activity and keeps management involved in it. The training department has each type of team fill out a brief registration form noting the team type, members and supervisor, and theme along with other information.

Teams also use identical forms for recording minutes of meetings, all of which are reviewed by the operations manager. At the end of a project, the team files a summary sheet or "storyboard" describing the improvements. A copy is attached to a suggestion form so the team can be rewarded. Supervisors verify results. Finally, each department has a group activity board where the minutes of projects are displayed and where the summary sheet is posted when projects end.

2. Support Activity

Suggestion System: The daily preproduction meetings stimulated increasingly sophisticated ideas so the company launched a suggestion system to log and test them. A training class teaches people how to fill out a suggestion form and how to identify waste. When people or teams come up with a better way of working, they clear the idea with a supervisor. Then they test it and measure the results.

Next, they fill out a suggestion form and submit it to the evaluation team which assesses the idea according to a point system within 60 days. Ideas are judged on originality, ease of implementation, and annual cost savings. The evaluation team awards up to 100 points, which can be exchanged monthly at a local department store for its in-store currency, Camrata explained. The evaluation team consists of representatives from human resources and representatives from each area in the plant.

Besides the tangible benefits of improvements in safety, quality, costs and efficiency, the company believes the suggestion system pays benefits that are tough to measure financially, but are valuable nonetheless. Among these are:

- Improving morale and motivation by letting people redesign their own work

- Recognizing the experience and knowledge held by employees

- Encouraging teamwork by involving supervisors, co-workers, and workers from other areas during implementation

Reward and Recognition: Besides the suggestion system, Aeroquip Inoac uses other forms of reward and recognition. The QC circles turn in summary sheets of projects to a review committee, which is a form of recognition, and a copy also goes to the suggestion system committee for reward consideration.

At an annual "presentation day," the TPM teams, action teams, QC circles, improvement teams, and other small groups, make presentation on what they have worked on to a panel of senior managers, who rate them on their application of the seven QC tools. "The presentations give people self-confidence and self-esteem," noted Jones. "You see a lot of pride here." All teams get an award. Two members from the top-rated team go to Japan for a companywide team competition.

Aeroquip Inoac's "level up" job classification system strongly promotes the continuous improvement culture by tying pay levels to participation. At level one, "we consider employees to be in training," explained Camrata. During this period they are "getting comfortable with their jobs" and going though a lot of in-house training.

When they reach a certain rate of pay, they advance to level two. "We start monitoring their participation" in teams and training, Camrata said. The company wants to see how often they offer suggestions, take training classes, or join teams such as the danger prediction teams. "We're not looking at the results, we just looking at their participation," she said.

To reach a level three rate of pay, employees must lead team activities. "You are not only involved with activities, but are leading activities of your own choice," Cheek said. For instance, an employee could lead a QC circle activity. "It's okay if someone just wants to come in and work their eight hours and go home," said Cheek. "That's fine." However, they would not advance to a level three rate of pay.

Roundtable Discussions: Discussion groups generally consist of six to eight people selected at random to sit down with the plant operations manager to discuss issues for one or two hours. Participants could include engineers, technicians, supervisors or team leaders. Managers hold roundtable discussions with hourly employees. The point is to expose any problems that may affect quality, cost, delivery, morale, or safety.

3. Education Activity

This includes a formal training effort and a "mentoring" process, explained Cheek. Classes cover a range of subjects such as applied electricity, aerial platform safety, the seven QC tools, and the basics of problems solving. Classes and registration forms are posted on a training board in each area. "It's all done on our time during work hours," she said.

Jones said the goal is to give every employee 40 hours of training. The plant's 659 nonunion employees make blow-molded plastic spoilers and some exterior trim in a 270,000-square-foot facility. The plant makes 28 different types of spoilers in 258 colors as well as service parts for customers such as GM, Toyota, Nissan, Ford, Mitsubishi, and Honda.

In 2001, it will begin making running boards for recreation vehicles and small trucks. The challenge for 2000 is to provide spoilers to customers by color and type in the sequence they will be installed. The culture comes into play in meeting the requirement. "One of the things about our culture is that we teach our people they have to be flexible because with continuous improvement comes continuous change," said Camrata.

Mentoring is a one-on-one teaching process that occurs at every level. It builds skills, trust and loyalty, and perpetuates the culture. Managers mentor rising supervisors, supervisors mentor up-and-coming team leaders, team leaders mentor team members aspiring to be leaders. Cheek said her mentor taught her by example. She would watch and "take tons of notes."

Training Within Industry (TWI) is a course that teaches supervisors how to help hourly employees in four key areas:

- Job instructions – how to teach and demonstrate a job to new employees

- Job methods – how to improve quality quickly with current manpower, machines, and material

- Job relations – how to respond to an HR problem.

- Job safety – how to analyze job procedures for safety and improve them.

At the end of the course, the HR department gives supervisors four laminated cards that serve as handy references on the shop floor. "It's like a reminder for them when they are instructing someone on how to do the job," said Cheek. "If they are not sure what to do next" supervisors pull out the appropriate cards to review step-by-step what to do. "They're very helpful," she said.

7 QC Tools: The kaizen culture never would have become concrete if employees, especially those on the QC Circles, could not collect and use data to solve problems. They learned how in a class on using the QC tools. First they learned how to make the charts and graphs, and then they brought data from their work areas to make the tools pertinent to daily work. Employees learn how to use check sheets, Pareto diagrams, cause and effect charts, scatter diagrams, histograms, control charts, and graphs of various kinds.

5S: The 5S effort, named for five Japanese words beginning with an S sound and roughly translates as Sort, Straighten, Shine, Standardize, and Sustain is aimed at turning the plant into a "showcase" for customers. The daily preproduction meeting often is dedicated to cleaning up the shop floor.

Management Activity

To change the typical middle manager's mindset, which is heavily influenced by cost accounting concepts, Japanese managers from Inoac mentored their American counterparts in the kaizen philosophy. Then the mentoring continued from American to American. Now, middle managers are mentored and trained in six key areas: creating a vision, general management skills, leadership skills, problem solving skills, human resource skills and communication skills.

TAKEAWAYS

- Use of small groups is an effective way to support lean culture.
- Training, education, and rewards and recognition are all critical to success.
- Managers must be trained as fully as all other employees.

5

Employees Offer Suggestions When a Process Is in Place

June, 2003

Employees were laid off in 2002 at the Sensormatic plant in San Antonio, Puerto Rico, because of the weak economy.

But even as that was happening, workers at the plant proposed a record number of ideas through the company's suggestion program. Those suggestions led to $1.7 million in savings — and that doesn't include about another half million dollars in cost avoidance, according to Luis Arroyo, director of advanced manufacturing engineering.

That result is testimony to the success of the suggestion program, which is a carefully structured, actively managed initiative at the 1,200-person plant.

The program, in turn, is one of a great many initiatives at the facility, where a commitment to lean principles has helped produce a wide range of benefits (see sidebar on p.35). The plant is a winner of the Shingo Prize for Excellence in Manufacturing.

While a suggestion program is only a small part of an overall lean transformation, it can play a pivotal role in motivating employees, building morale and achieving benefits. "The employee suggestion program is a vital element in helping us implement lean manufacturing," Arroyo says. "It makes it easier for us to implement major initiatives."

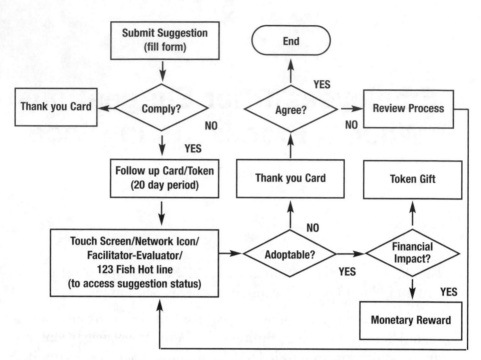

At the Sensomatic plant in San Antonio, Puerto Rico, suggestions are reviewed through a well-defined process.

At Sensormatic, the stated objectives of the program are to develop in associates:

- An attitude of loyalty and voluntary desire to bring about improvement

- An opportunity for individual expression

- A feeling that they have a part in the contribution of making Sensormatic a successful business

- A program that recognizes individual and team efforts

- A program that promotes the innovation and improvement of ideas generated by all Sensormatic associates, suppliers, visitors, family members

The program also has very specific goals that in 2002 included not

A Broad-Based Transformation

Among the other lean initiatives at place at the Sensormatic plant are:

- Training, Tools & Measurements, a continuous improvement method based on Motorola's Six Sigma Method.
- Organization of operations into nine internal business units, each with a multi-functional team and each operating as an individual business.
- TOCUSA, for Total Customer Satisfaction, focusing the business on delighting customers.
- Vendor-managed inventory programs aimed at reducing costs, reducing the size of the vendor base, establishing pull-based systems, eliminating waste and building relationships.

Major accomplishments, in addition to winning the Shingo Prize, include a doubling of injection molding capacity, space savings of 197,000 square feet, improvements in quality, workforce turnover of less than one percent, and what managers say is a transformation into a continuous improvement culture with a flexible factory and cross trained associates.

only achieving a certain level of savings, but also increasing participation of all associates by 100 percent, reducing suggestion response cycle time by 50 percent, and increasing the suggestion-per-associate rate by 100 percent and the percent of suggestions approved by 50 percent.

Structured Review

At its 265,000-square-foot plant, Sensormatic makes electronic security devices, including security tags and detection systems used in retail stores, and video and access control systems. The company is part of Tyco Safety Products.

The key to the suggestion program is a well-defined process for receiving and reviewing suggestions (see diagram on page 34). The process — as well other Sensormatic lean initiatives — was described in a presentation at last month's Shingo Prize conference by Arroyo and by Elliott Velez, quality assurance director.

After an employee submits a suggestion (by filling out a form), he or she receives a thank-you card within 24 hours, plus a voucher for lunch, worth about $3.50.

Suggestions are recorded in a database accessible through 450 computer terminals in the plant and also through what is called the 123 Fish hotline, so any employee can check the status of their suggestion.

If a review committee decides that a suggestion will generate enough savings to be worth adopting, then the employee will share in the savings. The employee receives a minimum of $25, and can receive up to $1,500, depending on the savings realized.

The employee is publicly presented with the check, and "we make a lot of noise," Arroyo notes. "We want to make the employee feel that he is the most important person in the company at that moment."

When the committee decides that an idea is not worth implementing, the employee can appeal. According to Arroyo, the employee wins the appeal about 60 percent of the time, "and they like that."

During the presentation, Arroyo described how the company tries to make it easy for employees to offer suggestions. Associates may write down suggestions in either Spanish or English. In some cases, a manager may listen to an employee and write down the suggestion on behalf of that person.

Administering the program costs the company about $20,000 per year, Arroyo said. Considering the savings achieved, not to mention the contribution to morale, that amount is "peanuts," he adds.

He also comments that his engineers spending 30 percent to 40 percent of their time reviewing and working with employee suggestions. "There's a lot of management support behind the program," he notes.

TAKEAWAYS

- A successful suggestion program must be carefully structured and actively managed.
- Goals can include the level of employee participation, the number of suggestions per associate, reducing suggestion cycle time and the percent of suggestions approved.
- Employees should be rewarded for making suggestions and should share in the savings achieved.

6

Approach Is Key in Attempt
To Make a Union a Partner

November, 2003

In 1992, the Lukens Inc. steel plant in Massillon, Ohio, was inefficient. Fifty percent of its finished product did not conform to specifications and had to be sold on the secondary market, half of all orders were shipped late, and costs were escalating.

Clearly, lean manufacturing could help. But to implement lean production, people must work together in teams, and the spirit of teamwork was hard to find. Relations between management and the workers' union were bitter from years of confrontation. Employees were trapped in a cycle of layoffs and rehires. The CEO of their former company was in jail for embezzling from the company.

Yet somehow, the Lukens workforce overcame these obstacles and successfully embarked on a lean journey. Within five years, yield and productivity were both up significantly, injuries were down and the proportion of on-time shipments regularly approached 100 percent.

The Lukens case is one of several situations that consultant Joel Smith says demonstrate lean manufacturing can be successfully implemented in union environments, even those with a legacy of confrontation and hostility.

As a senior consultant for Oriel Incorporated, Smith helped bring

How to Get Started

Key points in Joel Smith's Starting Points Checklist for working with a union on implementing lean production are:

- Start by putting a notebook together, document all you do.
- Informal discussion with senior union leadership: Make intentions clear, don't beat around the bush, offer to bring the leadership up to speed on lean.
- Stay away from making the process a bargaining issue.
- Agree bargaining issues will be addressed separately.
- Get input and thoughts from key managers.
- Form a small steering committee to get started.
- Jointly select outside facilitation help.
- Conduct Joint Leadership, Lean Education sessions.
- Establish a uniform problem-solving process.
- Rely on real data in decision-making.
- Conduct Joint Workshop(s) with key union/management leadership.
- Begin building a plan, use PDCA (plan, do, check, act). Establish goals, benchmarking visits to other companies, joint market studies, strategic planning.
- Chart information, identify trends, etc.
- Don't bite off more than you can chew.
- Communicate, communicate.
- Jointly identify key trouble spots where initial activity can provide successes. Use company & union data on attendance, safety, grievance load, production problems.
- Then find more confidence builders (opportunities for quick successes).

Smith also separately lists Executive Starting Points:

- Develop a partnership relationship with union counterpart.
- Spend some informal time together with union leadership.
- Senior union leadership should have access to executives, within a defined process (access and communication).
- Do not leave out or bypass lower-level management.
- You must be clear about intentions; use clear terms.
- Don't beat around the bush. Say what you mean and explain why.

together the two sides in the Lukens situation. Previously, as a representative for the United Auto Workers, he helped transform the GM Assembly Plant in Fremont, Calif. — which he says had a history of fights, drugs, booze, shootings and wildcat strikes — into what is today the plant operated by NUMMI (New United Motor Manufacturing Inc.), a joint venture of GM and Toyota.

"The key is to be open and honest about it, and another key is taking a risk — where you're willing to trust the other guy," Smith says.

Smith follows what he calls a Starting Points Checklist, a detailed agenda of what to do, and in what order, when trying to change union and management from adversaries into partners (see sidebar on p. 40).

Harder and Easier

Smith, who spoke at the recent conference of the Institute of Industrial Engineers in Atlanta, believes that union plants often are different from non-union plants.

"When you have real tough backgrounds, with a lot of conflict, in those environments it's pretty rough to get started," he says.

At the same time, he contends that once you get past the initial distrust, a union plant implementation is easier than one without a union. The reason, he maintains, is that with a union, the leaders of the workforce are clearly identified.

A critical point in building trust is keeping your word, he notes. "If you say you're going to do it, do it, even if it hurts."

Smith stresses that roles and responsibilities in a lean system must be clear and easily understood, they must be based on clear performance standards, they must impact every level of the organization and must involve labor and management working together.

Going lean, he says, begins with parties agreeing they want a better future, then jointly defining a future state model, jointly developing a plan to get there, and implementing the plan while continually checking and pushing.

Smith also believes that using an outsider to help bring labor and management together is a good idea, particularly if that person has experience that gives them credibility.

TAKEAWAYS

- When working with a union, process issues should be separated from bargaining issues.
- Taking the risk of trusting the other side is a critical step.
- Starting small, achieving quick successes and building relationships are fundamental.

7

The Really Tough Part: Selling Lean to the CEO

January, 2004

To get your chief executive officer to become a champion of a lean transformation, you need to:

- Get him to admit that other people may have better ideas than he does.

- Get him to accept that the way he's been doing things for years is wrong.

That's what must be done, and it's not easy, says Art Byrne, the widely respected former CEO of Wiremold, who drove lean change at that company for more than a decade. Most of the time, he adds, you won't succeed.

But occasionally someone does. And for those who want to try, Byrne offers some valuable advice about the role of the CEO in a lean transformation and how you can sell the CEO on its value.

"First and foremost, my opinion is that unless the CEO drives the change and is the champion for it, you have very little chance of success," says Byrne. "It's a very hard thing, huge change for an organization. If the CEO doesn't give his blessing, the chances that you will ever do it in a reasonable fashion are zero. The whole thing has to start with the CEO."

Byrne is currently an operating partner in J.W. Childs Associates.

He led implementation of lean practices at Wiremold from 1991 until 2002.

To drive change, he stresses, a CEO must understand that lean is more than cost-cutting.

"The key thing is, if you don't make it your core strategy, then you won't be successful," he states. "Probably 90 percent, maybe 99 percent of the people assigned to do lean think of it principally as a cost-reduction opportunity. They don't think of it as strategy, something that's core to what they do. They don't have any idea what's possible, and they don't understand how much they can get out of this.

"The CEO sort of has to be the evangelist for this program. It almost has to be a religious thing, where you run around saying 'I believe! Do you believe?'"

Much direction can come from the CEO, Byrne says, including establishing the metrics to be used and methods for follow-up. And there are specific steps that Byrne believes every CEO needs to take to transform the organization (see sidebar opposite).

It's also important that the CEO be aware of and involved in what is happening on the shop floor.

"Whenever I went to see any of my facilities, they all knew the first thing I wanted to do was take a walk on the shop floor. If nothing had happened (after improvements were planned), they know I'm going to see it," he explains.

Further, "even a good organization will slip backward," Byrne observes. "If the CEO doesn't sustain it — make sure that he doesn't have any backsliders, or is getting rid of them — it dies as well. This is something that takes years, and at any point in that time frame, you're subject to going backward in a big way."

Little Progress

But when a CEO is not already a strong advocate of lean, turning him or her into one can be a challenge. Says Byrne, "you're likely

Three Things Every CEO Should Do

To transform his or her company, one of the first things a CEO should do is "bring in a consultant," Art Byrne believes. "You can't be everywhere. A CEO just gets too tied up doing other things. You need a consulting effort for teaching principles."

However, he stresses you need consultants "you can rely on. You want ones that are going to teach the right principles. With a lot of guys, the reality is that what they are teaching isn't what Toyota is teaching at all. I've seen companies fall into that trap. They get the wrong consultants and get going in the wrong direction. You want not just any consultant, but someone really trained in, and who follows strictly, Toyota principles."

A second important step is to dedicate people full-time to continuous improvement. Byrne suggests that a company with 300 employees, for example, needs five to six people working full-time in what he calls a kaizen promotion office, or KPO. "An office should exist in every facility," he declares, "and the size of the facility and the business determine the size of the office. In effect, what happens with the KPO office is, you start with an external consultant, and you are training (the KPO staff) to be internal consultants. Every time the external consultant comes, the KPO office works with them and learns from them."

A KPO employee does not need to be knowledgeable about lean initially, but "needs to be a kind of change-agent type person, willing to try things, willing to experiment, not afraid of failing. They have to be pretty good with people: They have to talk the rest of the organization into trying something they think won't work."

A third, critical step is to reorganize the company, Byrne says. "Most organizations have a sort of functional organization. You have a foreman in charge of the punch press. People are functionally organized by machine type or type of operation. You want people aligned by product family. (At Wiremold) we had three product families. In the past, no one was really responsible for those families. They were never before responsible for making a product complete. One of the things that really helped was we put team leaders in charge of product families. We hold them accountable for the product, we hold them accountable for inventory turns, we hold them accountable for customer service. It's a different type of organization, but it simplifies what you are trying to do."

to find he will think of it in a narrow way, as cost reduction. To get him to think of it as a strategy thing, or a competitive weapon is pretty difficult. He'll have to do it for a number of years himself to make that change."

Byrne says his beliefs were reinforced at a Productivity conference where he led three roundtable discussions, each attended by about 10 people who were not CEOs.

"They're all basically in the same position, the same I would have predicted," he comments. "They're mostly people doing some stuff in lean. They got it kind of wrong. They're not exactly sure what to do with it. They've got it organized wrong, reporting to the wrong level. They can't get the guys above them to do anything. It's not the corporate culture. They're all kind of lost. They have this barrier, that barrier. 'Who do I get to take down the barriers for me?'

"I really think the number of people interested in lean and trying to do something is starting to go up. But the number that are doing it correctly or understand how to do it correctly is miniscule."

Selling Strategies

Lower-level managers trying to convince a CEO that a company should adopt lean practices face an uphill battle, Byrne is convinced, because a great many CEOs are not receptive to this kind of pitch.

He explains: "A lot of CEOs are very insecure. CEOs are no different from other people in that respect. They want to be in control all the time. To admit they don't know something, they might see as a sign of weakness. Sometimes it's hard to admit somebody below them is telling them something they ought to do. Most of the time it won't happen. Most of the time, the CEO at the end of the day says 'I'm in charge. No one can tell me what to do.'

"When I'm talking to CEOs myself, and I tell them what is possible, first I get this look: I don't believe you. They say, 'Why should I waste my time on something like that? Besides, I'm busy. I've got these other five initiatives I'm working on. Maybe three years from now, when I get done with all the stuff I'm doing now I can do it.' That's the general thing you get back from somebody."

Nonetheless, Byrne does believe that if a CEO is going to listen, another CEO is "probably the biggest influence." The CEO who is listening may ask "'why do I want to ignore this?' Then he sort of becomes the guy who initiates this. He'll say, 'my own people have been telling me, too, and I've been rejecting it, but maybe there's something to this.'"

And actual results are always good for convincing a CEO. "If somebody in the organization goes ahead and does a few things and gets results, now they can't deny it's happening in their own organization," Byrne suggests. "They can't say it wouldn't work here. If all of a sudden here in Division A, these guys are making huge progress with us, we should do this everyplace. It's one of the more powerful tools."

TAKEAWAYS

- The CEO must be committed to and involved in any lean transformation for it to succeed.
- Another CEO may be best able to influence your CEO.
- Hiring consultants, having full-time lean positions and reorganizing your company are essential.

8

"Semi-Stealth" Strategy Turns Top Executives Into Believers

December, 2004

You want to transform your company into a lean enterprise, but you don't have top management support. What do you do?

Quietly and thoroughly map the processes of one value stream, enlisting floor-level support along the way. Determine precisely which steps of those processes are value-adding. Clearly identify the benefits that can be achieved by eliminating waste. Then present your findings at a management meeting where you dazzle your superiors with your well-documented report.

"We were trying to stay below the radar until we were ready to present," says Russ Kalbfeld, who used just such a strategy at Sunstar Butler, a Chicago maker of toothbrushes and related products. "We felt if we could keep it at a low level, getting a lot of enthusiasm, then we could sell it to the next level up."

Kalbfeld succeeded. Lean is becoming an integral part of the way business is done at Sunstar Butler, which now has a senior engineer who works primarily on lean projects, a lean steering committee and a three-year strategy. The number of work cells is growing, employees are trained in lean methods, and the director of manufacturing will only support new operations if they are lean.

Equally important, in at least one product line Sunstar Butler has reduced lead times dramatically and achieved 100 percent on-time delivery for two years, with same-day service on 20 percent of the orders.

One Step at a Time

Sunstar Butler is a 700-employee company with annual sales of about $150 million. About 85 percent of its products are made at its Chicago facility. Kalbfeld is director of engineering at the company, reporting to the vice president of operations.

In 1998, problems were evident in the company's line of custom imprinted toothbrushes. These toothbrushes feature the name and phone number of the ordering dentist on the handle, along with a personalized logo. Imprinting is free if the dentist orders at least 12 dozen, and he or she can choose from more than 30 types of toothbrushes.

Dentists were unhappy with Sunstar Butler because they were being quoted delivery times of 8 to 10 weeks for the toothbrushes, but weren't receiving them for 12 to 16 weeks.

Kalbfeld had some experience with lean implementations from a previous job, as well as some training in just-in-time manufacturing through APICS. He believed that Sunstar Butler was a "perfect place" to apply lean principles.

But higher-level executives knew little of lean. His boss, the vice president of operations, was "the only one that semi-supported" his efforts, he says, and when it came to other top people, "we knew we were going to have to sell them on this."

So Kalbfeld began building support. Initially, his only cohorts were one of his senior engineers and an intern he hired in 1999. His charge to the intern — who was given a little lean training and who Kalbfeld says had good industrial engineering skills — was to "take an order that is shipping today and find out what happened, and why it took as long as it did." In other words, the intern was working on developing a value stream map.

The manager of the packaging department came on board, but

stressed that not all problems were within his department. "When we looked at it, he was right," Kalbfeld concedes. "The process took 12 to 16 weeks, and he was getting things done in a month."

The customer service department was involved, at the user level. "We went to customer service people and said, 'can you give us a few hours?' They were so open to it, it was amazing." Sales was brought into the effort, and members of Kalbfeld's team actually went out on sales calls to gather information. Marketing was also involved.

It wasn't actually designed as a consensus-building campaign. Kalbfeld comments: "When I think back, I would like to say yes, we had this great strategy. But the vision I had was to create a value stream map. The side effect of that was, we developed this internal support that became very strong."

Winning Everybody

The mapping process took six months. It culminated in a meeting with the Sunstar Butler operating committee, consisting of the president and all vice presidents.

"We did a very visual presentation, what I call the horizontal bar chart," says Kalbfeld, referring to the final value stream map, which wrapped around the meeting room walls, showing every segment of the 12 weeks it took to fill an order for the custom-imprinted toothbrushes.

Accompanying the map was a short line showing the actual value-adding time contained in those 12 weeks: two hours and 47 minutes.

"The VP of sales almost fell out of his chair," Kalbfeld recalls. "He said, 'you're telling me we can do all that in two hours and 47 minutes?' The VP of operations wouldn't go that far, but he said we could probably get it done in four to five weeks."

"At that point, we won everybody."

And so, Sunstar Butler began its lean journey, with actual implementation of improvements getting under way.

As is often the case in a lean transformation, "I can't say we found any one major catastrophic problem," Kalbfeld comments. "It was a host of little things."

For example, 50 percent of all incoming orders automatically went on to a credit hold while they were reviewed by the accounts payable department. "We lost several days just doing that."

There were other inefficiencies in the way orders were processed. Toothbrushes that had been imprinted would wait in a holding area before going on to packaging. Orders involving several different products would sit with just one product until the other products were obtained.

Many improvements were implemented. Several manufacturing cells have been created. A kanban system was established that streamlines the processing of multiple-product orders. The effort has begun to encompass other products, beyond the custom-imprinted toothbrushes, and Kalbfeld estimates "we're probably 30 percent done."

Today, the current average lead time on the imprinted products is five days.

The lean efforts are expanding. Improvement projects are targeting more products, and the new steering committee and three-year strategy are bringing it all together. "Our director of manufacturing is very strong on making sure this will continue," says Kalbfeld.

He concedes that his approach might be called "semi-stealth," and while the initial effort took six months, he is glad that it did.

"My boss certainly knew what we were working on, and how we were trying to go about it, but he didn't want to present it until we were ready," Kalbfeld recalls. "That was a good choice. If we presented too early and did not have all the facts, we could have lost that sale."

TAKEAWAYS

- All departments should be included in efforts to build floor-level support.
- The presentation to top management should be thoroughly researched and as strong as possible.
- A visually-oriented presentation can be highly effective.

Part II

Staff Development

OVERVIEW

Changing culture takes more than getting workers to support the concepts of lean. It takes workers and managers who understand the concepts, can develop strategy, know how to use the tools and know how to measure the results. In short, a lean culture must be supported by lean expertise throughout your organization.

A first step is to understand what skills currently exist among your workforce and how they need to be expanded. Chapter 9 is the first chapter originally published as a "Lean Advisor Q&A" column within *Lean Manufacturing Advisor*. This column explains the concept of a skills inventory, and how you determine what skills your organization has, whether they are adequate and whether they are up-to-date.

Chapter 10, also a Q&A column, zeroes in on the need for lean leaders. This chapter not only discusses how many leaders you may need, but how to use them to "seed" your organization so that a lean culture will grow and flourish.

In a related topic, Chapter 11 discusses how to recruit and hire lean leaders. Defining what the job of the leader will be, establishing the qualities you seek and then finding suitable candidates are all part of this highly informative discussion.

For those who find the recruiting and hiring process burdensome, Chapter 12 offers some unusual advice: Apply the concepts of lean to that process. As with all lean initiatives, doing so can help you make that process more efficient and more likely to add value to your organization.

Once you have lean leaders on board, you want to do everything possible to help them succeed. Chapter 13 presents some tips on how to do that; you will read here about 10 areas where supervisors most need help, and how you can provide it to them.

Helping its team leaders become all they can be is a priority at ESCO, described in the case study in Chapter 14. Top executives at ESCO put in place a plan that defined what a team leader does, what competencies he or she needs, the expectations that go with the position, and the training required to provide the necessary skills.

At Alfmeier, lean expertise is viewed as more than a contributing factor to lean culture. Officials there consider it a requirement for any high-level position within the company. And to make sure employees there have every opportunity to acquire the expertise needed to advance, the company offers its people a 15-module training program. Read about it in Chapter 15.

Similarly, United Plastics Group – the company described in Chapter 16 – established a team of lean coordinators not only to help transform the business, but to serve as a talent pool for management positions. While this means the company must constantly find new coordinators, it benefits from gaining managers with strong lean expertise.

It could be argued that a culture is built one employee at a time. The advice and case studies in this section offer insights that you can use to embark on that construction effort in your business.

9

Plan to Increase Your Skills Inventory

By
Richard Niedermeier
November, 2002

Our lean implementation is going slowly. We don't seem to have enough people to put the new methods in place, even though going lean should reduce the number of people we need for any given area. What's wrong?

A lean implementation usually means that inventory will be going down. But have you allowed for the skills inventory that should be going up?

When most production organizations look at implementing a lean approach, the focus is heavily slanted toward the financial impact of the inventory that will be turned into cash flow. The strategic targets of the organization are typically based on a conservative estimate of how much inventory will be reduced and the dollars generated. (Usually this is a fairly conservative number for the first several years as the organization begins to realize how much "excess" inventory was really there.)

But the financial impact of the inventory reduction distracts organizations from performing skill set inventories. Hold on to some of those inventory dollars. You're going to need them.

Count the Parts and the Skills

In the implementation plans that I have seen since 1987, more than two-thirds have no explicit program step to take a skills inventory of what the organization already knows in the way of methods, tools, and techniques. This can result in two different kinds of mistakes.

The first mistake is to assume that the skill already exists in the organization. Just as we take physical inventory to establish our benchmarks, you need to take a similar sort of inventory of the skill sets in the organization. The organization needs to find those people that have analytical skills and knowledge of methodologies and verify that these still exist. It is even more beneficial if the person who has the skill can teach others.

The primary thing to be sure of is that the skill sets required support the tactical plan as written both in time and in sequence. Having skills available too far in advance of their use is as wasteful as excess inventory. You find yourself paying for the skills far in advance of the benefit.

The second mistake that is usually made is that too few people are expert in the skill. The organization needs to find out how many people have certain skills and how many skill sets are already covered. If you're going to have a number of pilot initiatives underway simultaneously, you do not want to overwork those people who have the skills. It is better to train more.

If you do not have the right number of people with the given skill set, the implementation itself could stall. If this happens early in the implementation, it will reflect poorly and may discourage people from participating in the future. There are no hard and fast rules as to how many people need to acquire which skills. This is solely dependent on the sequence of the plan and its focus of improvement from one phase to the next.

Although the methodologies acquired may vary, there are some basic skills that are nearly always required. Most of the foundational skills are centered on teambuilding, team management, setting objectives, and managing meetings. In spite of the fact that these are relatively easy skills to develop, few companies invest the money in formal education for these skills.

Are They Current and Up To Date?

Most acquired skills need to be used to keep them fresh. If individuals who hold certain certificates in methods and skills received their education years earlier, they may need some practice or remedial education prior to use. Just like riding a bicycle, it may take some time to become expert at it again. Don't be afraid to get a trainer if you need to come up to speed quickly.

Save Inventory Money to Spend on Education

Only half of most organizations have budgeted dollars for training and education. The inventory reduction dollars are taken to the bottom line and flushed out of the balance sheet of the company. Organizations must allow a budget for training and education as part of the implementation program. Even those organizations that do go through the process of establishing a budget for it find that the dollars allocated are usually inadequate to accomplish the task. Be sure that the quotation information being used is current. Raw material is not the only thing that has gone up in cost.

TAKEAWAYS

- A skills inventory can help determine what skills your organization has, and which it needs.
- Skills must be used regularly to remain fresh.
- The budget must include funds for training and education.

Acquiring and Building Expertise

By
Linford Stiles
October 2003

We are starting a lean journey and don't have any lean experts in-house. What kinds of people do we need, and how many?

In addition to senseis and other visiting lean experts, you need experienced people as employees within your organization. These "Lean Leaders" have done it all before and recognize the pitfalls. They are not afraid to shut down the line, get to the root causes or insist that there will be no return to the old way (something inexperienced people tend to do at the first sign of a problem).

I strongly advocate "seeding" the organization with people who have been successful adopters of lean at another site. Their experience should include basic training in a credible lean program where they were guided by a lean expert and encouraged to experiment in a team environment. They should have worked with most of the lean tools and participated in deploying lean policy.

It is all right if many of your seeds have not experienced leading a lean conversion without heavy oversight. However, successful change experience should be a part of the background of the top "seeds." A small cadre of these people — coupled with sensei advice — will almost guarantee long-lasting change.

The sensei will provide the initial impetus and strategic direction for improvement. The internal lean experts will make sure the new methods are sustained and gradually will take over leading ongoing improvement. It is a process that, over time, eliminates the need for outside expertise. A good sensei recognizes this and will insist on progress toward that goal.

Total Involvement

How many experienced people are required? That depends entirely on a company's size, enterprise involvement and ability to digest change. A single plant operation concentrating on manufacturing change might require only three experienced people, one leading the two others. A company seeking to implement lean across the entire enterprise (accounting, engineering, sales, etc.) might need a leader for each of these areas.

Bear in mind the end game. Many companies have progressed to the point that these pre-existing "silos" have been dissolved, replaced by cross-functional teams, each with full capability of managing its own business unit. One of our clients, a $14 billion company with a worldwide presence, discovered that its original eight businesses could be more effectively managed by converging and collapsing them into four and maintaining complete business control.

Many companies make the mistake of forgoing the previous step and instead immediately confer the title of "lean change agent" on a promising employee. They hope this person will quickly acquire the skills to lead this charge to continuous improvement. It rarely works. This is not the fault of the designated ones (although they frequently receive the blame). There unfortunately is much more to this simple-looking process than the uneducated observer can predict. In these cases, opportunities for gains are lost and most likely will not be available again for some time.

It is important to water the "seeds" with praise and instill recognition of the need for "critical mass." For lean success, the entire workforce must accept and buy into the effort. Everyone (or at least a significant majority) must feel a part of the movement and a contributor to continuous improvement. Three lone people in a plant of 300 cannot hope to convert the thinking of the other 297 and gain support.

There must be a feeder program that continually brings trained and enthusiastic supporters to the front line. The company needs to organize training that teaches the principles of waste removal. The seeds and the outside consultants can be of great value here. As improvements free up people, don't lay them off or fire them. In fact, most of our clients take the most promising candidates from service and place them in training, leaving those who have still to make up their minds about lean on the shortened line. Many companies find that attrition and retirement more than make up for the need to reduce staff. At all costs, avoid layoffs directly resulting from lean improvements.

TAKEAWAYS

- People experienced in lean should be hired to "seed" an organization just getting started in lean.
- A lean leader may be needed for each area.
- Trained and enthusiastic supporters should continually be moved up in the organization.

11

Plan Your Search Carefully to Get the Right Lean Leader

December, 2004

If you want to hire people who will be lean change agents within your organization, you need to know what types of people you are looking for and where to find them.

That means you must define the job responsibilities and qualifications, then actively recruit people who fit that profile.

And perhaps surprisingly, "lean skills are not at the top of the list" of qualifications, says Adam Zak, managing director of Adams and Associates International, an executive recruiting firm that specializes in lean positions. "Leadership is really the most important."

Zak stresses that any job search must begin with an internal needs assessment. Questions to be asked include:

- Why do we need this person?

- Where are we in our lean transformation?

- What, therefore, do we want this person to accomplish?

- On that basis, what are the candidate selection criteria?

Overall, "what you're after is someone who takes a holistic approach to lean," he says, meaning someone who seeks to transform an entire enterprise, not just apply lean tools to one area.

While it is easy to say that leadership is the most important quality of any candidate, Zak also believes that quality must be defined. He believes a leader is someone who:

- Is a charismatic persuader who can bring passion to the organization

- Is participative and leads by modeling behavior

- Knows what he or she needs to know

- Has the ability to identify, assess and harvest opportunities that others fail to see

- Makes decisions from strong personal beliefs and values (courage)

- Finds commonality of purpose with the team

Communication is next on Zak's list of qualities for a lean change agent. He also defines this quality in detail, with aspects ranging from making people and knowledge accessible to others, to creating effective experiences that build cultures, to engaging people across enterprise boundaries.

Coaching and motivation skills are also an important attribute.

Relevant Experience

In some areas, one definition does not fit all. For example, the lean technical and functional skills being sought will vary from company to company, depending on the position requirements. A staff position may involve different skills from a line role.

Virtually every company requires that a candidate have a degree, as a lack of one will limit the person's potential for advancement. "Technical degrees are usually in top demand," Zak notes, but he adds that Japanese language majors are also very popular.

Speaking of Asian countries, Zak observes that China "has become, and I believe will continue to become, a major customer for lean." He notes that his firm is currently involved in 27 lean searches in China, many at a "very senior level."

Ultimately, experience is more important than degrees. But in evaluating experience, many questions should be asked, Zak says. Issues to be considered include:

- Whether the candidate's industry experience is relevant and transferable

- Whether he or she has experience in a company of similar size and scope

- Whether the person has demonstrated fast-track advancement

- How much kaizen experience the person has (with the related question, how many kaizens are enough?)

- Which consultants the candidate has worked with

Zak urges employers to beware of "kaizen kowboys," "tool-time techies" and "workshop wonders" – people who may have some limited or focused experience with lean techniques but whose experience lacks depth and who may not have a broad understanding of lean principles and goals.

Multiple Strategies

Finding lean candidates can be difficult, partly because demand for them is increasing. Zak notes that lean searches in healthcare are currently strong, as well as in process manufacturing industries. In addition, in what he says is a surprise, demand has surfaced during 2004 in the retailing, energy and pharmaceutical industries. "They've awakened to the fact that something like lean will be important to them," he concludes.

Zak recommends using multiple strategies. Networking is always important, and his advice is to "connect to your personal network."

He also believes in pursuing direct competitors as well as lean players in similar industries. He cautions, though, that some companies with a reputation for being lean "are not as lean as you'd think." And he notes that there are different "styles" of lean, plus varying degrees and quality of lean implementation. The key question, he states, is whether a candidate's experience is transferable to and sustainable in the searching company.

Another option is to go where lean people go: lean conferences. Zak's conference list includes the Productivity, Inc. annual conference (where he spoke in November, 2004), the conference and workshops of the Association for Manufacturing Excellence, activities at several universities, and events of the Society of Manufacturing Engineers.

However, he cautions against becoming an industry "pariah." He explains: "If you go to too many conferences and try to recruit too many people, you'll become a persona non grata."

And as a final warning, Zak urges companies to screen all candidates carefully. Why? Studies have found, he says, that more than 40 percent of all résumés contain some inaccurate information, and more than 25 percent have material misstatements.

TAKEAWAYS

- Internal needs should be assessed before a lean position is defined and filled.
- The skills that are needed will not be the same for all lean positions.
- Multiple strategies are necessary to find lean candidates.

Improving Hiring Processes Saves Both Time and Money

December, 2002

In a survey of hiring practices at more than 100 companies, executive recruiter Adam Zak found only two that religiously followed a structured interview process and performance-based criteria for evaluating candidates. And each of those companies went through an unusual experience.

Each was scheduled to interview eight or nine candidates for a particular position. In each case, the second candidate interviewed met or exceeded all of the performance criteria. And in each case, the company offered the job to that candidate (who accepted) and canceled the rest of the interviews, "thereby saving considerable expense and dramatically shaving cycle time for these hires," Zak notes.

This was possible, Zak stresses, precisely because the hiring decision was based on objective criteria and not on emotion, opinion or personal bias. More broadly, use of such criteria can be part of applying the principles and concepts of lean production to the recruiting and hiring process, saving time and money as well as increasing the likelihood of hiring the right person.

Zak, managing director of Adams and Associates International, a Barrington, Ill., recruiter specializing in filling lean positions, described the survey, as well as ways to improve hiring and recruiting, at Productivity's 8th Annual Lean Management and TPM conference, held in Nashville. In describing how the two companies mentioned above shortened the interview process, he asked the audience "Are you bold enough, and confident enough in your performance-based criteria to follow their lead?

Where Waste Exists

Zak's survey found that hiring and recruiting processes are frequently plagued by the seven types of waste identified through applying lean principles. Examples include:

- **Overproduction.** Poorly designed advertisements bring in many responses, including many unqualified candidates, causing HR staffs to waste time going through inappropriate résumés. This also creates risk that good candidates will be missed in the screening, or lost to other jobs by the time they are finally called.

- **Waiting.** Hiring decisions are delayed by waits for documentation or internal approvals, and by delays in obtaining references. These delays cost money, as a good lean manager can immediately help the company find new savings.

- **Transportation.** Travel – when you visit a candidate or transport them to you – is waste when it's the wrong candidate. And improper sequencing of recruiting events can cause unnecessary transport of documents overnight.

- **Overprocessing.** Advertising must be repeated if the wrong companies are targeted at first, and interviews may have to be repeated if the process drags out too long.

- **Inventory.** Maintaining a database of more resumes than you need takes time and costs money, and it may cause you to rely on the database when you should be looking for new candidates.

- **Movement.** Unnecessary motion to find information that wasn't properly filed means information may get lost, the process may be delayed, and it may cost more.

- **Defects.** A bad process means you hire the wrong person. Zak notes that this is the one form of waste companies will not tolerate; every other form of waste is acceptable, so long as a good person is hired.

Improving the Process

The companies that have established the best recruiting systems, Zak says, did so by having a solid vision of where they wanted to go, created a strategy to get there, tied tools back to the strategy, rolled the strategy out throughout the organization, "took frequent course corrections" and had support from top leadership.

He also stresses the importance of fact-based metrics to provide clarity, standardize evaluation and help change behavior.

A metrics scorecard can include:

- New-hire performance
- Manager satisfaction
- New-hire satisfaction
- New-hire failure rate
- New-hire turnover rate
- New-hire time to productivity
- Candidate sourcing quality
- Candidate interviews per hire
- Offers accepted vs. turned down
- Time to hire
- Cost per hire
- Yield (quality of candidates meeting hiring manager expectations)

A team approach is valuable, Zak says, and the team's initial role is to analyze needs and determine how success or failure will be measured.

It is also important to create forms and checklists, timetables with deadlines, a standardized matrix for defining important criteria, and so on. While this can be a lot of work, "over time they will save you time and money by helping you error-proof the process," he states.

Developing an effective recruiting system can help you anticipate needs and hire in a pro-active manner. The issues to be addressed by such a plan include:

- How many new employees you will need in the year ahead.

- Why – and when – they will be needed.

- How much it will cost to hire them.

- What value they will bring to customers and the organization.

Interviews should be structured to remove subjectivity, and candidates should be evaluated based on performance-based criteria. For an example, Zak suggests, a candidate might be asked to describe a situation where he or she employed 5S techniques, specifically focusing on what the person did and what resulted. The answer would help interviewers to judge the person's level of vision and business savvy, he states, and how that individual would fit into company operations.

A performance-based job profile is essential, Zak says, spelling out the essential activities each person must accomplish and the outcomes he or she must deliver to get the job done. This "sets the tone for the entire process and dictates specific decisions and actions at each step of the process," he explains, from the kind of candidate you seek to the selection of a search firm to the questions you ask in interviews.

To create this profile, it can be helpful to review past appraisals to see what works and what doesn't, talk to both internal and external experts, do qualitative benchmarking and determine what the person must have accomplished after a given time period.

Additional issues include whether to use a search firm, any forms of outsourcing or other strategies, such as internship programs; developing an effective screening system; preparing fully for interviews; checking references thoroughly; developing criteria for selecting finalists, building offers and closing the deal.

Eye on the Prize

Zak had wanted to use the results of his survey to develop what he calls a "composite current state and future state value stream map for the recruiting process," but he notes that none of the companies responding to the survey was willing to share its entire process in detail.

But by focusing on the above issues, he maintains, a company can increase the odds of hiring the right people, generate consistency in hiring decisions, support people development, improve benchmarking and reduce the cost and cycle time in the hiring process.

He comments, "you can't make immediate and wholesale changes in the quality of your people. You can establish behavioral benchmarks and standards within your hiring process. Over time, as you start hiring to those standards, you gradually improve the level of talent in your organization."

TAKEAWAYS

- Job candidates should be screened with a structured interview process and performance-based criteria.
- Not all candidates must be interviewed, if one who meets the criteria is found early.
- A team approach is valuable.

13

Ten Critical Areas Where Supervisors Need Your Help With Culture Change

July, 2001

The cultural change needed for a successful lean transformation has to happen at the shop-floor level of workers and first-line supervisors, notes Ron Grundhoefer, a former supervisor.

It's "absolutely important" that management look at supervisors and hourly people as customers during the change process, said Grundhoefer, who spent 7 of his 31 years in Alcoa management as a supervisor. "To me that's what is going to drive a lean organization -- being the resource, being available to give them help when they need it." And supervisors need help nowadays. Just look at the job description:

- Motivate the mediocre, boost the morale of the burned-out, and decrease pressure on the stressed-out.

- Delegate but remain responsible for any outcome.

- Be task-oriented for upper management and people-oriented for employees.

- Foster cooperation and a team spirit among prima donnas.

- Set departmental goals that are out of reach, yet not out of sight.

- Reinforce employee productivity with diminishing resources.

- Maintain open communication without wasting time with chit-chat.

- Squeeze more work into a shrinking amount of time, using less money.

"That's a very, very difficult path to walk," says Grundhoefer, who is now a consultant with Productivity, Inc. "I know it was for me."

In addition to these expectations, supervisors play a critical role in a lean transformation. They are the crucial links between the management hierarchy and the people who put their hands on or put their minds to the real work of the company. Supervisors can "bridge the gap" between the current culture and the desired one, notes Grundhoefer.

Despite these complex expectations, most organizations give supervisors limited attention. Education for them is usually on-the-job training, says Grundhoefer. But to foster a successful cultural change, supervisors need the organization's support to be effective in 10 key areas:

1. Mini-business manager

2. Team leader

3. Team coach

4. Self-developer

5. Workplace manager

6. Safety manager

7. Customer satisfier

8. Supplier developer

9. Upward relations manager

10. Technical specialist

1. Mini-business Manager

"It's absolutely important that you allow them to manage their own business," says Grundhoefer. Managing means setting a vision, values, and goals aligned with those of the company but relevant at the shop-floor level. Supervisors also need the budgeting and cost control skills to manage the work unit as if it were a business.

Shared values or team norms serve as the "rules of the game" of how people will work together to achieve the objectives of the business. Grundhoefer suggests involving team members in defining values that are in-line with company values. Once agreed, everyone should "walk the talk."

Although the transition will take years, Grundhoefer cautions you to set the shop-floor goals no more than "6 to 12 months out."

2. Team Leader

Supervisors need the knowledge and skills to lead and motivate an outstanding team. Grundhoefer offers a four-stage change model for supervisors to follow:

Stage 1: Establish the need for change
1. Create dissatisfaction with the current state.
2. Involve the team in developing the gap between the ideal and the present.
3. Build support for change by key individuals on the team.
4. List and communicate the benefits of change to the team.

Stage 2: Plan the change
1. How to move from the present to the ideal.
2. Involve the team in planning.
3. Pinpoint responsibility.
4. Communicate the plan to all.

Stage 3: Lead the change
1. Initiate the first steps to the change.
2. Reward and recognize change efforts.
3. Communicate early success.

4. Show empathy and caring to the people affected by the change.

Stage 4: Review progress and sustain the gain
1. Review progress of the plan to achieve the desired end result and replan if necessary.
2. Develop standard operating procedures to ensure that new skills and behavior are sustained.
3, Confirm and communicate.
4. Communicate achievements.

3. Team Coach

"This is usually an area we bypass," Grundhoefer says. "We just make the assumption they know how to do that. That's a bad mistake." Acting as a coach will seem "strange" to most supervisors, Grundhoefer predicts. Most don't do a good job coaching because management hasn't given them the training. Coaching to many supervisors means control. Actually, it requires the supervisor to:

1. Lead

2. Get people involved

3. Communicate, which consists of:
   • Effective presentations
   • Effective meetings
   • Effective listening
   • Acting as a leader not a boss

Coaching also requires supervisors to develop the skills of the team and its members by:

   • Exposing people to situations in which they learn about teamwork

   • Giving broad goals and allowing participation in target setting and methodology

   • Supporting the team to develop its own way of working

   • Leading by example

- Measuring progress and providing positive feedback

"People need and expect feedback on how they are doing," says Grundhoefer. "It should be going on all the time." Therefore, there should be few major surprises during the appraisal meeting. If there are, the appraiser has not been doing his or her job properly during the preceding months.

4. Self-developer

This is the ability to learn more about yourself and your capabilities; "to take charge of your own destiny," says Grundhoefer. A self-developer:

- Responds positively to information or criticism, and works to improve

- Remains objective in all situations

- Works continuously to improve interpersonal skills and leadership skills

- Demonstrates a positive attitude toward himself or herself, team members, and the company

- Takes initiative and responsibility for his or her own growth

- Displays innovation and is open to change

- Responds with patience and confidence in a crisis

Supervisors should take the time to "get some feedback from their peers" on how well they meet these behaviors.

During the beginning of Alcoa's lean transition in 1991, the company sent Grundhoefer and 50 other people, including many first-line supervisors, to get masters degrees in applied behavioral science. Why? So they would have the people skills needed for the cultural change. They learned how to deal with issues like conflict and change, and how to evaluate themselves in order to develop high levels of personal competence.

5. Workplace Manager

Supervisors must know the lean manufacturing tools, such as 5S and TPM, so they can identify and eliminate waste. They must be able to develop management techniques on the shop floor aimed at improving quality, cost, delivery, safety, and morale (QCDSM). The supervisor must:

- Conduct benchmarking to compare performance against world-class performance.

- Apply workplace improvement techniques aimed at improving QCDSM.

- Investigate the facts and fundamental causes of problems and take corrective actions.

- Create a positive, competitive team spirit.

- Ensure that standard operating procedures are followed and displayed.

Grundhoefer describes standard operating procedures (SOP) as a formal written document that includes all information about a task including its description, main steps in the right sequence, key points, and the reasons for those key points. It cites the required protective clothing, equipment and tools used, necessary checks for quality and safety, and the training needed. It also states the time allowed to do the job.

Because the SOP details the current known best method for doing a job, any deviation from it will jeopardize quality, productivity, or safety, he notes.

Once a task has been standardized, it can be improved. Therefore, the SOP is the starting point for all improvement activity. Once new methods have been implemented, the standard operating procedure is updated. This is a form of continuous improvement.

"Operators ought to own the SOPs," Grundhoefer says. "They will help maintain what they help build."

6. Safety Manager

Many organizations have made a lot of progress in this area by giving supervisors the knowledge and opportunities to analyze and improve safety within their work areas. The key points in this area are that supervisors must:

- Know all health and safety rules, procedures, and standards.

- Work continuously towards improvement of safety standards and work areas.

- Inspect the work area regularly.

- Investigate and report the true facts and fundamental causes of accidents.

- Model safe work procedures.

- Take corrective action to prevent re-occurrence.

- Train team members.

7. Customer Satisfier

The supervisors and their teams must know who the internal and external customers are, what they want, and when they want it. "Involve the team in solving problems that your customer might be encountering," he says. "And, by the way, if you're on day shift and another crew is coming in on afternoon shift, they would also be considered your customer," Grundhoefer notes. Supervisors should sit down with them and ask what their requirements are. They should also:

- Realize that the process is also a customer and motivate the team to do the same.

- Display a positive attitude towards the customer and expect the same from the team.

- Meet regularly with customers to understand their needs and seek ways of improving product and services.

- Keep promises; deliver on time.

- Listen to and fully understand customers' needs and adjust to changing needs or priorities.

- Measure customer satisfaction and plan improvement.

8. Supplier Developer

"This is another key performance area that the supervisors in a lean manufacturing organization have to get very, very good at," says Grundhoefer. People who work in internal areas that supply front-line supervisors, such as maintenance, stores, and engineering, must have positive relationships with them. "Too often, there is a tremendous amount of blaming going on," says Grundhoefer. Supervisors in a lean organization:

- Communicate requirements and standards clearly to suppliers.

- Understand supplier needs.

- Provide continuous feedback to suppliers and support groups.

- Develop procedures or systems to monitor quality of products/services.

- Involve and help suppliers to improve their products and services.

- Measure supplier service and plan improvement.

9. Upward Relations Manager

To ensure the effective functioning of their mini-businesses, supervisors must be effective in dealing with upper management and keeping it informed about what is going on. "Too often this doesn't happen," says Grundhoefer. "It's been my experience that the reason it doesn't happen is that we tend to fear authority." The effect is that people don't want to ask questions or provide feedback to our bosses. Supervisors also must be able to:

- Take the organization's goals and bring them down into the team or department.

- Develop good interaction skills with his or her boss.

- Understand the priorities and main objectives of his or her boss.

- Support management even if unpopular decisions need to be implemented.

- Protect and build the assets of the mini-business.

- Identify problems before they occur.

- Support and model the change initiative.

Supervisors should not just go to their managers with problems. "Go to them with the problem and recommendations," Grundhoefer says.

10. Technical Specialist

Supervisors must have the technical knowledge from process expertise to problem-solving tools that are needed to do the job. In addition, they must:

- Have opportunities to further develop their technical competence.

- Identify, analyze, and solve problems.

- Apply problem solving tools and techniques such as check-sheets, Pareto analysis, brainstorming, control charts, histograms, and fishbone diagrams.

- Have process and technical knowledge of the mini-business.

- Transfer technical and process knowledge to team members.

As a final piece of advice, Grundhoefer challenges middle and senior managers to "discipline yourselves to spend a minimum of one or two hours a week walking around the shop floor talking to supervisors and shop-floor people. Find out what's going on. It's much easier to not do this. We'll find all kinds of reasons not to do this."

TAKEAWAYS

- Supervisors and hourly workers should be viewed as "customers" of the change process.
- A supervisor fills a variety of roles, and may need help with all of them.
- Training and feedback are the essential elements of the help to be provided.

Structured Program Builds Skills of Team Leaders

December, 2003

While lean manufacturing offers many tools for improving business processes, there's no single best tool or method for improving the skills of team leaders. Yet every company on a lean journey needs to build leadership skills because of the critical role team leaders play in driving improvements.

Because of that, ESCO Corp. in Portland, Ore., has developed a highly structured program for creating outstanding team leaders by clearly defining responsibilities and expectations, providing ongoing feedback and rewarding accomplishments.

It is a program begun in 1997, and one that has evolved since then, with refinements to development plans and reviews, for example. It is also a program that managers say has improved morale, increased trust among all departments and raised standards, not to mention helping to improve operations.

"I really believe that whether you are trying to focus on the people side or if you are trying to work on the business or process side of improvement, those have to be tied together somehow. Neither one can function on its own," says Aaron Koehler, manufacturing manager.

Koehler, director of organizational development Elizabeth King and team leader Mark Waggoner describes ESCO's efforts at the

2003 annual conference of the Association for Manufacturing Excellence, held in Toronto.

Structure and Details

ESCO makes engineered metal parts and components for industrial machinery. The company employs approximately 3,500 people in four business units, and the development plan was created at its foundries in Portland.

The need for such a program stemmed from the fact that, in 1997, "we needed to grow people and we needed to do it now. We were downsizing, people were retiring, and we didn't have people ready to fill in and take their jobs," Koehler recalls.

Initially, ESCO tried to reinvent the wheel. "We spent about six months trying to create something original, and we were falling really short," he admits. "We decided to chuck it all out and start again."

The second time, the company utilized materials from Lominger, a Minneapolis-based provider of training and organizational tools, and consulting services. The company's materials provided a basis for the ESCO program.

The company has established three levels of team leadership. To clarify the roles and responsibilities of people at each level, the program handbook includes:

- Definitions. These are essentially job descriptions of the three levels of team leaders, listing the number of years experience typical for each level, skills expected at that level and some responsibilities. For example, a Team Leader 2 has been a team leader for five years, "is effective in motivating and developing others in a team environment," "works with outside vendors to ensure material availability and inventory control," and "is recognized as an expert within the department." A Team Leader 3 typically has 10 years experience, "develops others by assisting manufacturing

Cross Training PDR Form, for: _____Mark W.____ Date: May 22nd, 2002 | Sample |

Business Objectives

- **Communication Between Departments**
  What measures can Finishing provide to Pouring which will allow pouring to improve their quality? Where and how should they be compiled? What scrap decisions can be made earlier in the process?
- **Visual Work Instructions**
  Review the standard work instructions. Evaluate each for effectiveness accuracy, and clarity. Provide written feedback about each.
- **Departmental Measures**
  What is being measured, and are they the right things to measure? Are there other measures that would be meaningful to workers in this area?
- **Process Flow**
  Learn what the Departmental goals & objectives are, and how they fit into the P3 process flow. Look for ways that Pouring / Shakeout can make the job easier/better for finishing. This is to include a nightly walk thru the plant with (at least) Jim M., looking at the effects of Molding & Pouring on quality and scrap.

Leadership Skills (all available in FYI™ Book)

- **Managing & Measuring Work**
  This is a chance to improve a needed skill in a different Department. In Finishing we are looking at how many oven skips of work we can process a day. Look at ways you can help here, and what you can take back to Pouring.
- **Decision Quality**
  Become comfortable making good decisions, in uncomfortable circumstances.
- **Patience/Composure**
  These are skills that Jim M. is very good at. As you know, Jim is very willing to share his experiences. Try to observe and practice some of these good behaviors. Document what you've tried, what worked, what didn't.
- **Presentation Skills**

Technical Skills

Finishing Department

Flogging Operations	complete
- Skip loading	
Ovens	to be done week of 6/24
- Equipment	
- Scheduling	
- ISO Requirements & MII'S	
Sawing Operations	
Grind & Fitting Operations	to be done week of 7/1
- Gauging	
Re-work	
- Welding	
- ISO Requirements & MII'S	
Inspection	
- Visual	
- MT knowledge-	
- ISO Requirements & MII'S	to be done week of 7/8
- Gauging	
- Count out & P/P	
Crane Operation (optional)	
Fork Lift Operation (optional)	
Dept. Admin	
- Time sheets	all to be done by 7/12
- Absentees	
- Basic understanding of equipment	
- Oracle Transactions	
- Dept. Measures	
- Corrective Action Resolution	
- Trouble-shooting	

Presentation to Team Leaders

Title: What were you able to accomplish with additional time?

Date: At first T.L. meeting after training is complete.

This cross-training form is one of the documents ESCO uses in evaluating and guiding team leaders.

manager in employee evaluation and training," can fill in for the manufacturing manager and "is considered as an expert and corporate resource in his/her field."

- Competencies. These are divided into three categories — managing yourself, managing the team and managing the business — and each team leader level has specific competencies listed under each category. For example, under managing the business, Team Leader 1's competencies are decision quality and functional/technical skills. Those for Team Leader 2 are customer focus, problem solving and process management. The list is longer for Team Leader 3 and includes drive for results, negotiation, organizational agility, planning, presentation skills and reengineering.

In addition, the program also includes:

- Expectations. There is one set of expectations that is the same for all three levels. Each of the expectations, which are listed below, is described in more detail within the program.

  - Support and promote management goals.
  - Support and help implement change.
  - Develop and use standard work procedures.
  - Fix it now.
  - Self development.
  - Employee development.
  - Support team members and peers.
  - Kaizen involvement.
  - Lead by example.
  - Meet production goals.
  - Enforce safety requirements.
  - On-time and accurate time reports.

- Training and Development. This includes:

  - Leadership training, based on materials from Interact Performance Systems of Anaheim, Calif. The four-part training focuses on communicating the problem situation, solving motivation problems, solving ability problems, dealing with emergent problems and refining and extending problem-solving skills.
  - Peer/360-degree evaluation from a leader's boss, peers and direct reports.
  - Individual development plans, created jointly by the team leader and manufacturing manager.
  - Cross-training.
  - Performance development reviews.

– Team Leader trainee program for people who are not yet team leaders.

Cross-training in particular has been a significant development of the team leader program. Those involved say it broadens skills, increases flexibility and gives leaders greater opportunity to advance.

Individuals receive specific percentage pay increases for advancing to team leadership. And since advancing from one leader level to the next can take time — moving from the first level to the third can take 10 years — there are additional opportunities for pay increases while a person is still within a given level.

Full Steam Ahead

The team leader program is one part of a broader focus by ESCO on lean initiatives, which also include using tools such as 5S, standardized work, kanban systems, a focus on takt time and initial efforts to apply 3P (pre-production planning).

According to King, certain parts of the program are now being used throughout ESCO's other business units.

Since the effort was launched, ESCO has gone through some challenging times due to the down economy, including some staff reductions. But development of the team leader program and other lean efforts continued "full steam ahead," King says. Koehler adds, "regardless of whether the economy has affected us in an up or down condition, this work brings us a lot of benefit in either condition."

TAKEAWAYS

- Each level of leadership should have a job description, listing required experience, skills, responsibilities and competencies.
- Expectations must be established, and appropriate training must be provided.
- Pay increases should be awarded for advancing to a higher level.

Want a High-Level Job Here?
You Better Learn Lean First

July, 2004

The best way to build your next generation of top executives is to train them in lean principles.

That's what Alfmeier Corporation believes, and that's what the company is doing. Thirty-five employees of the Greenville, S.C. manufacturer are nearing the end of what Alfmeier calls Gemba Black Belt Certification, an internal two-year management development program that will make the students eligible for management or leadership positions that open up in the future.

Alfmeier has been on a lean journey since around 1997, but the new training program — this is the first group of employees to go through it — was launched after the company conducted an internal analysis.

"One of the weaknesses we identified is that we did not have a feeder system (for future leaders)," notes Dean Davidson, vice president of North American operations. "We did not have any bench strength."

The program consists of 15 modules, each built around a lean tool or principle — 5S, the Toyota Production System, kanban, policy deployment, and so on. The training for any particular module takes from half a day to four days and occurs mostly outside of regular working hours. The program was designed internally; some training is conducted by Alfmeier managers while consultants and local technical colleges are used for other modules. "It would have slowed down the program trying to do it all ourselves," says Davidson.

Each student must complete and graduate from each module. Following completion of the modules, each student must undertake an improvement project, the results of which are reported to upper management in a storyboard format. If a student successfully completes that project, with upper management satisfied the student has learned and is proficient in all lean concepts, the worker is awarded certification, receives a bonus and enters the pool of leadership candidates. Eleven of the thirty-five students are currently in the project phase.

Finding the Right People

Alfmeier is a German company with annual sales of about 120 million euros. The Greenville operation, which now employs about 200 people, was launched in 1994. It serves the automotive market, making engine systems, fuel management systems and seating comfort products.

Davidson and other lean veterans were hired to help run the Greenville plant. Their success implementing lean production gradually spread throughout the company, as early wins convinced top management that lean was the way to go. "We ended up leading Alfmeier worldwide through a lean transformation. The momentum started here in North America," recalls Davidson. He has since traveled overseas, to countries including Germany and the Czech Republic, to provide lean training.

"I think the hardest part of the training was to get them to see the need for the training itself," he comments. "After we would do one example of value stream mapping, and through that example, we would see inefficiencies in whatever area of the company we had selected to work on, it became very obvious to people how much more there was out there. But the initial surge, the initial interest, it was 'why am I in this training?' Breaking the ice was the toughest part."

In contrast, one of the more challenging parts of the new Gemba certification program is not breaking the ice, but selecting the right students.

"You identify your lean leaders," Davidson explains. "Some people will get it, some won't. You don't have to fuel the fire. They just go back to their work area and start practicing lean. Those are the people you try to pull out and identify as future leaders."

Once they are chosen, he adds, "we make sure they know what we see in them. Their behavior, their way of talking. 'You like this stuff don't you?' You have that conversation. You try to find out what is their interest, what do they want to do for the company. We develop that progression path for each individual. We as a company look for opportunities to help them get there." The 35 chosen for the certification program had "fire in the belly," he declares

But it takes more than that. According to Davidson, a lean leader must be visual, data-driven, action-oriented, experienced, instinctive, passionate, confident, unassuming, an effective communicator, a process coach, relentless, fearless, a perfectionist, and his or her company's toughest critic — among other attributes.

Davidson also argues that top executives must be trained to be lean thinkers and held accountable for implementing the lean vision — no exceptions.

And to get the whole thing going, he says, "you have to create a crisis. You have to have a crisis on top of you, or you create one, and you create a sense of urgency for having a lean journey. It may be financial — you have competitors coming in, you are no longer the lowest cost producer. You need some kind of initiative and tools to get your competitiveness back. Otherwise, this initiative could be perceived as the flavor of the month. Most companies have a crisis. That's not the hard part."

TAKEAWAYS

- Lean expertise should be a prerequisite for high-level posts.
- Providing training can help develop new leaders.
- Not everyone is suited to a leadership position.

16

Plastics Firm's Lean Team
Is Its Source of New Talent

November, 2002

Less than a year after hiring five people for his team of lean coordinators at United Plastics Group, Chris Sigmon has had to replace all of them.

That's because the five coordinators were hired not only to help make the injection molding company lean, but also to serve as its talent pool. "We knew we wanted to make changes," Sigmon notes.

All five still work for UPG, but have moved on to other positions. One is corporate materials manager, another is corporate tooling manager, and the three others are an operations manager, a quality manager and an engineering manager.

That's not the end of the lean team, however. Sigmon has hired four replacements and is seeking a fifth.

All this was by design. Just as injection molding machines form plastic into products, a number of executives and venture capitalists molded several small plastics firms into UPG, based in Westmont, Ill. From the beginning, in 1998, their plan was to eliminate duplication and waste to create one efficient company. Hiring of coordinators who serve as management prospects was part of the broader effort to create one business with one culture dedicated to lean manufacturing.

That effort has already taken the company nearly halfway to its target of $20 million in annualized savings, with $9 million achieved so far. In addition, four facilities have been closed, though a new plant has been opened in China.

(In announcing the opening of the China plant in September, 2002, a UPG news release said the facility in Suzhou is "one of the few manufacturing facilities in the world to encompass lean manufacturing principles from the ground up.")

United Plastics — which has about $270 million in sales and about 1,000 employees — claims to be the first plastics manufacturer to fully implement lean manufacturing across all its facilities (11 in total). A company news release says that in addition to reducing costs, the year-old lean initiative has also decreased time to market, decreased manufacturing cycles and increased productivity.

Mining the Gold

UPG was created in 1998 when Aurora Capital, a venture capital firm, decided that opportunities existed in the injection molding business. The firm bought five small plastics companies, then spent the first few years forming them into one business and getting a management team in place.

"Clearly we had redundant systems in place. We had several different cultures, companies functioning as independent silos," Sigmon says. He was brought on board in 2001, with a lean background gained in the automotive industry, into the position of vice president of business integration and UPG production systems. Half of Sigmon's job is to integrate large amounts of business into the facilities — using capacity planning, for example. The other half is to focus on improving production systems, primarily through lean manufacturing.

Sigmon describes the five acquired companies as "Rip Van Winkles — they slept through the lean revolution." That creates opportunities: "We walked into Fort Knox. I say that there's gold laying on the ground of every plant we went into."

Building expertise — through hiring skilled people and through training — has been a key strategy in mining that gold, along with what Sigmon calls a "shotgun and rifle" approach.

That involves a focus in three areas, the first two of which Sigmon classifies under "shotgun." Initially, every employee receives training in the UPG production system and the basics of lean manufacturing, in a four-hour course. Since the program began, the company has trained almost all of its employees.

Second, more detailed training is provided to each facility's general manager — a UPG "survival kit," Sigmon says, with "Cliff Notes on all the different programs we have." Goals and objectives are established, and bonuses and incentives are aligned with those goals.

All this establishes a common language, Sigmon says, and gives the general managers tools to achieve improvements on their own.

At a third level, "the lean coordinators are our rifles," Sigmon says. Each coordinator is required to be able to teach and implement 5S and a kanban system. However, each then may have greater expertise than the others in a particular lean area — designing a cell, for example. If a facility is pursuing a project in that area, then the knowledgeable coordinator serves as a resource.

Sigmon notes that he recently hired a coordinator with skills in using software for modeling what a facility should look like — expertise no one else on the team has.

"There has to be a common understanding within the organization, so that everyone understands the benefits. At the same time, there have to be project-specific, focused workshops to go along with that," he says.

In addition to aligning incentives and goals for managers, Sigmon says UPG has also had to work to eliminate competition between plants. "Everyone's goals and objectives are tied to performance and overall company performance. Company performance has to come first," he says.

At the same time, specific lean initiatives typically are launched within individual plants, rather than company-wide. Each plant manager is a "cowboy," Sigmon jokes, with "complete autonomy to run their plant as their own business."

Strategies for Success

One of the largest savings achieved so far was $5.8 million from the elimination of 361 jobs. That runs counter to the usual practice in lean manufacturing, where employees are often promised that their efforts won't lead to layoffs. Otherwise, they may not support the transformation.

However, Sigmon notes that the reductions so far have been of temporary workers, who are widely used in the industry. "We really haven't cut into our full-time workforce," he says. "That's a luxury we have. We are getting down to that level. We will try to do it [further reductions] through attrition."

Other benefits include reductions in work-in-process, reductions in scrap, faster changeovers, and reductions in floor space of as much as 50 percent in some facilities. In a plant in the Chicago area, Sigmon says, the workforce was cut by 40 percent while on-time delivery improved, defects dropped by 30 percent, required floor space was cut in half and the plant maintained the same level of sales. The company is now trying to sublease the freed-up floor space.

The current efforts, which Sigmon sees as grabbing the low-hanging fruit, will be followed by what he calls two evolutionary steps. One will be to apply Six Sigma techniques to technical processes, through the hiring of a lean coordinator with a Six Sigma black belt. Second, lean initiatives will be extended to UPG's supply chain, to both suppliers and customers. Some customers "have no clue what lean manufacturing is — I'd love to take a coordinator into their facility," Sigmon comments.

While he emphasizes the alignment of goals and compensation, and the shotgun and rifle approach, Sigmon stresses that to make lean succeed, "the key factor for me is dedicated resources. It's very difficult to do this, to take people out of a full-time job.

"Second, you need a management team that knows that your direction is correct. I've seen so many companies get analysis paralysis. They try to justify everything along the way. If you know it's the right thing to do, then let's go ahead and do it. Don't get caught up in the details of cost tracking."

And when first getting started, he says, "you want to get out of the box with wins. Don't bite off more than you can chew. When you are selling to employees, make sure your first projects are home runs."

TAKEAWAYS

- Moving people from full-time lean positions to other posts spreads lean talent through a company.
- Every employee should receive some lean training, with specialists receiving advanced training.
- Compensation must be aligned with corporate goals.

Part III

Sustaining Change

OVERVIEW

For a series of lean initiatives to become a genuine lean transformation, one that weaves lean into the very fabric of how you do business every day, you need policies, processes and procedures that have lean as an integral part of their DNA. You also need ways to communicate with and involve your workforce in lean activities on an ongoing basis. The chapters in this section offer suggestions on ways to achieve those goals.

One preliminary question is to what extent your culture is already lean – which can indicate how much further you have to go. Chapter 17 describes a tool for assessing your culture – a relatively simple device, but one that can provide valuable information.

Chapter 18 lists a series of what are essentially ongoing management activities designed to build consensus and maintain support for a lean approach. This straightforward list is focused on TPM efforts, but is applicable to virtually any aspect of lean.

Communication with employees is an essential part of sustaining lean culture, and perhaps no other company is more active in providing feedback than O.C. Tanner. How this manufacturer manages to evaluate employees every two weeks is the subject of Chapter 19.

Improving communication is also the focus of Chapter 20, which discusses how to have the best possible daily production meeting. The information in this chapter can guide you to a meeting that not only gives your workforce better information, but also provides surprisingly strong support to your lean efforts.

In addition to effective communication and feedback, employees need to be compensated in way that supports your corporate strategy. Chapter 21, another Lean Advisor Q&A column, explains how to structure compensation in a manner consistent with a lean approach.

Similarly, the performance incentives offered to workers should also further your lean goals. Those incentives are the focus of Chapter 22, which notes some common mistakes companies make in structuring incentives, offers some practical advice and describes the approach taken at the Flexible Steel Lacing Company.

Chapter 23 tells the story of how The Bama Companies, a winner of the Malcolm Baldrige National Quality Award, improved business processes through the unusual approach of focusing on employee satisfaction. By addressing employee concerns, Bama not only boosted morale, but boosted its own business results.

And Chapter 24 explains how McKesson Canada took the improvement methodologies it had been using to make production processes better and integrated them into every aspect of operations, from management decision-making to project selection.

Lean is a never-ending journey, and sustaining lean culture requires never-ending diligence. The chapters in this section provide insights into where to focus those ongoing efforts to make your transformation successful and lasting.

17

An Assessment Tool Tells You Whether Your Culture Is Lean

October, 2004

Have you transformed your corporate culture to the point where it will support and sustain lean initiatives? One way to answer that question is to use an assessment tool that evaluates the state of your culture.

Kevin McManus, of the Great Systems! consulting firm in Seattle, has developed one such tool. He believes that a supportive culture "is the difference between a program of the year and a process that is integrated into the 'fabric of the organization.'" An industrial engineer, McManus comes by his views as a result of more than 20 years working at a variety of manufacturing organizations, in positions ranging from production manager to plant manager to director of quality. He has also been an examiner for the Malcolm Baldrige National Quality Award since 1998.

The heart of any assessment tool is the set of questions being asked. McManus' tool consists of 30 questions, 3 in each of 10 categories, with each question to be answered by a rating of from one to six. McManus is the first to say that each category focuses on "the three things that I feel have the greatest impact on making that area work."

For example, one category is Job Design, and the first question in that category is "To what degree do jobs include time for project work?" The answers range from "only engineers and some managers" (worth only one point) to "most members of management" (in the middle of the scale) to "majority of employees" (six points).

If the assessment yields a total of from 136 points to the maximum possible score of 180 points, you're in good shape, McManus says. He divides possible scores into a total of four assessment levels, and says the lowest (45 points or less) means "your lean effort is destined for the 'program of the month' graveyard."

In addition to Job Design, the other categories of questions are Leadership, Compensation, Communication, Planning, Training, Process Management, Measurement, Technology and Customer Satisfaction.

Within the categories, many of the questions focus on whether processes and metrics are in place to support a lean transformation.

For example, one Leadership question is "To what degree is lean support a performance expectation?" Answers range from "they have been asked to do this" to "support is measured." Similarly, the Compensation section asks whether lean contributions are formally recognized, with answers ranging from "only when the dollars are great" to "we do this monthly."

The Process Management section asks to what degree all key processes are defined and trended. The lowest answer is "production processes are defined" while the top score is awarded when "all are defined and trended." A question under Measurement asks how many teams use balanced scorecards. All teams using scorecards brings the highest rating, while the lowest score is given when there is only a company scorecard.

McManus points out that the tool can be used not only for an overall assessment, but also to identify particular problem areas.

Getting From Here to There

Of course, if your culture doesn't measure up, an assessment tool by itself only hints at ways to make things better.

McManus offers what he sees as key action plan items for improvement in seven categories:

Compensation. Modify compensation plans to support lean progress, and use the time savings to grow the business, train and develop projects.

Leadership. Clarify expectations for the behavior of key leaders, and measure leadership styles and consistency.

Planning. Use one process for managing all key projects, and gauge progress with to-date and future timelines.

Training. Practice modeling effective lean behaviors. Teach people what a lean culture looks, sounds and feels like.

Feedback. Reinforce positive performance frequently, and make sure internal customers share expectations.

Measurement. Use a balanced approach and put success in "dollar" forms whenever possible.

Transformation. Redesign and improve every job. Recognize and reward lean success in a fair manner.

He also suggests additional actions that can be taken to move your transformation forward. For example, he proposes using technology as a lean catalyst, with its benefits including reducing process costs, sharing lean efforts and successes, and identifying and verifying lean opportunities.

McManus also believes in building strong customer links, particularly with internal customers. He proposes regular meetings toward development of a shared vision and shared expectations.

His overall slogan is "change systems to shift cultures."

He states: "Systems change shapes and shifts a culture, and the more people who help make this happen and in turn take ownership in the effort, the greater your probability of success will be. More people equal more emotion, and with the right systems in place, you are in a much better position to ensure that the emotions you generate will be highly positive, as opposed to largely negative."

18

Nine Steps for Getting TPM Buy-In From Varied Groups

December, 1999

A lot of groups must buy in to your TPM effort for it to be a success. The key ones include employees, supervisors, and, if applicable in your facility, union officials. Ronald Grundhoefer, a Productivity TPM consultant who previously worked at Alcoa for 31 years, holding posts ranging from front-line supervisor to manager, offers you these nine steps based on his experience with TPM and organizational change. They are aimed at helping leaders develop a process for change beginning with direct reports, and maintaining a balance between authority while encouraging employee autonomy and participation.

Step 1: The Leader Leads

The leader sets the course and stays the course in a non-reactive way against the inevitable resistance, often expressed as:

"It can't be done…"

"We tried this before…"

"All of us should decide…"

"I got a better idea…"

"What's in it for me…"

Keys

- You will need a balance between authority and consensus.

- You will need to balance business objectives and employee initiatives.

- Remember there is no freedom without structure.

Step 2: Align Direct Reports

The leader meets with and shares TPM goals with direct reports, helping them to align with the goals. The objectives should be stretch goals, critical to the organization and achievable in 6 to 12 months. Listen to reports' concerns, but don't allow them to veto the direction of the organization.

Keys

- The organization's direction is not a consensus decision or majority vote.

- Tell reports it is safe to disagree, but it's not safe to be unsupportive of your decision after an airing of differences.

- Allow them the opportunity to have input on the "how to" portion of implementing the change.

- Be clear.

Step 3: Communicate With Union Officials

Share the goals with union officials. Tell them "what" you will be doing, and "why." Stress the importance of successful implementation and the consequences to the organization of failing to implement. Inform them you will be communicating your goals across the plant or organization. Let them review what you will be communicating to the workforce.

Keys

- Don't surprise them.

- Tell them the truth, don't hide information.

- Ask for their help and support.

- Ask for their input on "how to" accomplish the goals.

- Expect push back.

- Expect possible bargaining.

Step 4: Communicate Goals Across the Plant

Communicate your goals to the workforce across the plant or department in small group meetings. Talk about:

- The global picture.

- The competition.

- The things you can control such as safety, costs, and quality.

- Describe your bottom-line goals, work processes, and people goals.

- Tell them the "ball is in our court."

Keys

- Don't let the negative people dominate the conversations and meetings.

- Tell them the "whats" and "whys."

- Deliver your message with simple clarity.

- Be prepared for "push back" but stay the course.

Step 5: Meet With Salaried Leadership

Have meetings with key salaried leadership, including the first-line supervisors, to develop alignment with your goals by having them translate your goals into objectives for their work units.

Keys

- Instruct leaders to cascade the goals to their work groups.

- Let them know who decides what, who does what and by when.

- This is a critical step because the real day-to-day "sponsor" of the TPM effort will be each and every employee and the employee's boss.

Step 6: Leaders Cascade Goals Down to Work Groups

Have each leader cascade the goals down to their work groups. The leaders of each work group will meet with their people and communicate their unit's role in the effort. Leaders will need to have dialogue about the need for clarity concerning deadlines, decision-making, throughput, or whatever is blocking groups from achieving their unit's goals.

Keys

- At this step, you must make sure the boss-employee relationship shifts to leader-leader relationship where everyone assumes leadership towards achieving goals.

- Each unit will need several additional sessions to see what's working well and what isn't. Constant follow-up sessions are necessary.

- Involve union leadership in getting necessary support for change.

- Remember: real culture changes happen at the floor level.

Step 7: Work With Groups to Insure Clarity

This basically deals with three questions. Bringing all three to a high level will insure success.

1. How skilled is the leader in interacting with others?

2. How much clarity is there among the team members about the various tasks?

3. How healthy is the work system overall?

Keys

- The leader must constantly support individuals, groups, and managers/ supervisors in formal and informal conversations about "how's it going?"

- Expect breakdowns of agreements, work relationships, role understanding, and work processes.

- Keep an eye on production projects that need to be accomplished to achieve your goals.

- Be prepared to give leaders additional training if needed.

Step 8: Train Key Individuals as Change Agents

Train and develop key individuals who have high interactive skills such as the capacity to take a stand, be decisive, stay the course against resistance, and keep connected.

Keys

- Training should consist of such subjects as: achieving goals, accountability, conflict resolution, decision-making, coaching, and problem solving.

- These key individuals could be both hourly and salary.

Step 9: Observe, Evaluate and Implement the Change Process

Stay firm about your goals, but flexible about your process. Remember leaders flip from being authoritarian to being permissive and then back to authoritarian when permissiveness doesn't work. Try to find the path or balance between the extremes.

Keys

- Establish and track key measurables.

- Audit the change process – have meetings, tours, one-on-one talks, etc.

- Remember the leader leads with a clear vision, stays the course, stays connected to employees, and is authentic. He or she must be decisive, listen with empathy, and avoid extremes.

TAKEAWAYS

- A leader must balance authority and consensus, freedom and structure.
- Communication and training are fundamental parts of building buy-in.
- Goals at various levels must be aligned, and leaders cascade goals downward.

Frequent Feedback Fosters Changes in Company Culture

February, 2004

To transform a traditional company culture into a lean culture, you need to educate your work force and train them in lean methods and tools. And you have to constantly reinforce what you have taught.

The O.C. Tanner company has a unique way of providing that reinforcement. They evaluate employees not just once or twice a year, but every two weeks.

"It's all about expectations," says Paul Terry, vice president, supply chain. "If you want alignment of your people, working toward the company mission, the way to get people dialed into that is to clearly communicate what goals and expectations are. The whole essence of what we are doing is that people know what to expect."

The evaluations — based on a detailed evaluation form that has evolved over several years (shown on page 114) — are part of a comprehensive lean strategy that includes everything from a team-based approach to extensive training, from manufacturing cells and kaizen events to employee recognition and rewards. It's a strategy that helped the company's main plant in Salt Lake City win the Shingo Prize for Excellence in Manufacturing in 1999.

"Our greatest success as a company is that we have an empowered workforce now," declares Harold Simons, vice president of

Team Member Evaluation

Team Member:	Team #	Date:

5) Always tries to find better ways to do the work. Helps the team improve.	Optimize order fulfillment
4) Often tries to learn and work better. Is proud of work.	
3) Usually is interested and tries to do new things. Wants to learn when there is an opportunity.	
2) Does only the work she/he has to do. Almost never tries to do better work.	
1) Never tries to learn or get better.	
5) Has excellent relationships with people, even in a hard situation. Does more than she/he is asked to do to help the team succeed.	Great place to work
4) Always polite and helpful. Works well with the team.	
3) Usually helps and is polite. Has a good relationship with other people. Wants to help the team in their work.	
2) Sometimes doesn't want to help the team. Is often impolite or angry. Doesn't help the team work better.	
1) Hard to work with. Doesn't help. Makes the team work slower.	
5) Learned or is learning to do all usual job responsibilities very well. Can learn harder skills without problems.	Skilled employees
4) Does all usual work well. Can learn harder skills with help and training.	
3) Ability to do the job is acceptable. Learns some harder skills. Flexes to help the team or other areas as often as needed.	
2) Facilitator or team members has to tell him/her what to do. Doesn't want to learn harder skills.	
1) Didn't learn or isn't learning job skills. Instructions always have to be repeated so she/he can finish the work.	
5) Always has the highest quality. The highest possible production rate.	Optimize order fulfillment
4) Careful and correct. Almost never makes mistakes. Higher than average in productivity.	
3) Work meets quality standards. Almost never passes on a product with a defect. Production rate is acceptable.	
2) Sometimes isn't careful. Makes the same errors many times. Usually does not meet expectations – makes the team slower.	
1) Makes many mistakes. Often work is not finished. Does not meet expectations – stops the team.	
5) Never misses work except when the absence is covered and scheduled before. Always comes to work on time. Always returns from lunch and breaks on time.	Capable & committed employees
4) Very good attendance. Is on time. Is dependable and does what she/he should do.	
3) Good attendance. Usually on time for work and returning from breaks. Usually dependable.	
2) Needs to improve. Often misses work or comes back from break or lunch late.	
1) Very poor attendance. Often late to work. Is not dependable.	
5) Uses different ways to solve easy and hard problems. Watches the solutions, decides if they are right and changes them if necessary.	Optimize order fulfillment
4) Can see problems. Can see what causes the problems and finds ways to solve most of them.	
3) Can see problems. Tries to find solutions.	
2) Doesn't see problems, doesn't see what causes them. Doesn't try to solve problems.	
1) Acts or talks like she/he is a victim of the problems and can't do anything to solve them. Does not see problems as a chance to make things better.	
5) Follows all safety rules. Always tries to help team members to be safer. Uses close call tickets to report unsafe conditions or actions.	Great place to work
4) Follows all safety rules. Tries to help team members to be safer.	
3) Follows all safety rules.	
2) Usually follows all safety rules. Sometimes needs to be reminded about safety rules.	
1) Does not follow all safety rules. Does not take safety seriously and/or puts the safety of others at risk.	
5) Consistently Contributing Ideas Towards Company Vision. Value Stream Focus is Evident, Helps Other Team Members.	Capable & committed employees
4) Some Effort to Improve Department to Align with Team/Department/Company Vision.	
3) Understands and Follows Company Initiatives…Lean, Teams, Standard Work, Continuous Improvement, Kanbans	
2) Agrees with Company Vision, but Struggles to Follow It.	
1) Does not Agree with Company Vision. Has Own Agenda.	

If a Team Member has a 2 or lower in any area, an Individual Coaching Plan must be in place.

Coach Signature: _____ Team Member Signature: _____

manufacturing. "It's definitely different from what we had eight years ago."

It seems fitting that O.C. Tanner credits its success to its workforce, since the company is in the employee recognition business. O.C.

Tanner makes everything from jewelry to sports equipment for corporate recognition programs. It also administers recognition programs and can help its customers publicize them to employees. The manufacturer employs roughly 2,000 people; about 1,600 work in Salt Lake City.

Like many companies that embark on a lean journey, O.C. Tanner has traveled through a complete transformation of its operations and its corporate culture. And while that transformation is evident in manufacturing methods and strategies, it is perhaps most pronounced in the training, evaluation and development of employees.

An Evolving System

O.C. Tanner first tackled lean manufacturing in 1998. That effort led to the first changes in management practices, but not the last.

The company was shifting from batch-and-queue manufacturing to cells, and cells were set up with three consecutive areas of manufacturing. Cross-functional teams were created within each area. Eventually, the three areas were combined into one, where each cell took production from beginning to end.

To match these changes, O.C. Tanner began cross-training employees so that each would have a range of skills to perform all functions with a team's area. Training cells were created, where new employees spent several weeks mastering fundamental skills before actually beginning work on the shop floor.

In addition, the company set up a system of pay increases so that a worker would receive more money each time he or she learned a new skill.

However, several aspects of that new system have since been replaced. For one thing, the training cells have been eliminated. Terry explains: "As we get leaner and leaner, and teams get smaller, we are really better able to handle cross-training challenges within the team. Now we mentor people. A new person comes straight into the team. They are buddied up (with an experienced person). Since we check-do-verify at every step, we are not worried about quality problems being passed on. It's a better way to orient new people."

The compensation system has also evolved. New employees come in at a lower pay rate until their skills match those of more experienced workers. But increases for veteran employees are no longer tied to gaining additional skills because a majority of workers are now cross-trained. O.C. Tanner has reached the point where the primary focus is less on teaching people about lean and more on achieving its benefits. Today, workers receive semi-annual pay increases. The amount is within a certain range and depends on performance.

Rewards and Recognition

The company also rewards employees in a variety of other ways. For one thing, every hourly employee receives what is called a QED bonus twice a year, based on O.C. Tanner's success in achieving its goals of quality, efficiency and delivery. In 2003 the two payments have totaled about $1,000.

In addition, individual employees can be nominated by peers or managers for performance awards. If a nomination is approved by management, the employee may be eligible to select a gift from one of the company's categories of gifts. The gifts range in value from $50 to $1,000, depending on the achievement. For example, Simons says, a manager in a gold refining lab received a $1,000 gift for developing a 10-karat gold alloy that was more tarnish resistant that 14-karat gold.

"Almost daily, somewhere in the company, one or two people are receiving performance recognition," Simons notes. "It could be a dozen on some days."

And there are other types of rewards. When a maintenance crew worked weekends for a while to deal with special problems, some received performance awards, but they were also taken out to dinner. When a team completes a kaizen blitz, its members will typically be taken out for lunch — wherever they want to go, Terry says. Employees have received boxes of chocolates for Thanksgiving and a turkey or ham at Christmas.

"We treat people pretty darn well," Simons boasts.

He notes that an O.C. Tanner executive spoke in China, and found himself speaking with Chinese government officials. They expressed interest in having western executives teach government leaders of manufacturing how to recognize and reward employees because that approach "is so foreign to their culture," Simons says. "Government factories are losing people to private factories. Even the Chinese government is saying we've got to recognize people and take care them and make them feel good about what they are doing."

TAKEAWAYS

- A detailed evaluation process helps communicate goals and expectations, and empower employees.
- Training and incentive systems should evolve over time as a company matures.
- The evaluation process should include clear steps to be taken in the event of a poor evaluation.

20

A Good Day of Production Begins With a Good Meeting

January, 2005

You may have set up cells, created a kanban system and applied 5S to organize your workplace. But have you improved your daily production meeting?

John Boyer believes you should. The head of consulting firm J.E. Boyer Company, in North Ogden, Utah, he contends that often companies either fail to have daily production meetings or conduct them poorly.

The result, he says, is "communication tends to be incomplete, priorities get out of order, and a lot of times, the factory will just become a law unto itself, and kind of go do what they want."

Having a good daily production meeting is particularly important with lean initiatives, Boyer adds, because "in a lean environment, it's very important to have an output rate set. It's important to check regularly. The daily production meeting is the formal and accountable forum for doing that.

"For example, when a daily production meeting is done correctly, there will be a document that contains the work that's supposed to be done in that cell on that day, organized in due-date sequence. It is rate-based, per the agreed-upon output rate of the cell. A lot of times, companies haven't quite thought about organizing their information in that kind of way."

Success Factors

There are several other factors necessary for a good daily production meeting, Boyer maintains, and the first one is **management commitment.** Top management needs to make clear that the meeting will be held and is mandatory for all involved.

Identifying who should be involved is the next step. Typically, the meeting participants include the production manager, line supervisors, schedulers, sometimes a materials person and sometimes a customer service person. The production manager "owns" the meeting.

A clear agenda is also required, and Boyer says the agenda essentially consists of two parts: reviewing performance of the previous day and discussing the outlook for the next couple of days.

"Next we need to have agreed-upon, **simple performance metrics.** Normally the two main ones are 'did we hit the rate?' and 'did we hit the schedule?'" he notes. "There is usually some kind of quality metric, a safety metric, and sometimes productivity."

After that, says Boyer, the information for the meeting must be in what he calls "fit for use" condition, meaning "the production schedule that organizes what the cells are going to run, by cell, in ascending date sequence, and it is leveled to the agreed-upon rate of output."

When the meeting actually takes place, he observes, "a lot of people will post performances," typically on a whiteboard.

That posted data can become available to other groups. For example, in addition to daily production meetings, some companies have regular cell meetings, at which members of a cell team will review the same types of information, but specific to that cell.

At the meeting, all order dates – customer order, production order and purchase order – are updated (and must be valid).

Interest and Impact

Boyer has 30 years experience in manufacturing and consulting. A frequent conference speaker, he spoke at the 2004 annual APICS conference about improving the production meeting to what he said was one of the largest groups ever attending one of his talks.

He attributes that to the fact that "every manufacturer I've ever walked into attempts to do this. I never found anybody right out of the box who was really very good at it. It's just something that nobody ever taught anybody how to do."

Quantifying the benefits of an improved meeting may be difficult, though Boyer suggests the most measurable outcomes are improvements in schedule and output rate performance.

He believes that when the meeting is better, "communication improves. Accountability is better. The whole process of communicating and understanding when things are going to be done is much better dealt with, and the real beneficiary of that is the customer." In addition, he says, problems are more likely to be anticipated and dealt with more rapidly.

He concludes, "Getting the daily production meeting straightened out is extremely simple to do, it doesn't cost hardly anything, and it's a high impact thing to do."

TAKEAWAYS

- A good daily production meeting clearly establishes expectations for that day's output.
- Management must make clear that participation in the meeting is mandatory.
- Identifying who is involved, a clear agenda and simple metrics are all necessary.

Compensation Helps Lean Pay Off

By Kevin McManus

December, 2004

What compensation system changes or additions are needed to support a lean initiative over time?

Whenever you try to implement any significant improvement strategy, such as lean manufacturing or the lean enterprise, you will come up against the "what's in it for me?" question. If you have a plan for modifying your existing compensation system as your strategy begins to pay off, you will stand a much better chance of both sustaining the improvement effort and getting more out of it.

There are four key compensation approaches that need to evolve in concert with any successful improvement initiative - the compensation package itself; the way in which employees are kept informed about improvement progress versus business performance; the process that is used to formally recognize employees; and the way your leaders say 'thank you' each day. Most organizations have some form of each of these approaches in place already, but they may not be designed to support a lean implementation.

The compensation package. For example, having a sound, fair profit-sharing plan will help sustain your lean efforts. With such a plan, employees receive some form of scaled bonus for better results, and the line of sight between personal efforts and the compensation for such efforts is short (ideally monthly). The paycheck is the primary way people gauge compensation fairness and represents the most consistent form of performance feedback. When the paycheck reflects the effort that was expended to try something new, a sense of both pride and ownership is fostered. An 'unfair' paycheck — one that does not change even though money is being saved or significant personal changes have been made — raises questions of unfairness, and acts as a de-motivator.

Keeping employees informed. Providing your workforce with regular updates on the lean successes being realized and how those successes impact the bottom line further fuels this sense of pride and ownership. Monthly 'all hands' meetings, bulletin board postings and newsletters are examples of ways to recognize individuals and teams that have made key contributions or met key performance standards. The monthly meeting forum in particular can be used to draw a direct connection between what their personal efforts cost the company that month in compensation and the amount of money those efforts saved. As this connection is reinforced over time, the level of business literacy in the company will grow as well.

Employee recognition. Individual and team contributions can also be recognized monthly, or on an ad hoc basis, with rewards for 'above goal' or special contributions. Gift certificates, clothing and free food are some of the more common types of this form of recognition. Be careful to avoid recognizing individual contributions at the expense of the team or performance in certain areas as opposed to any area where superior performance was observed. This practice does not motivate as much as it sends a strong signal to the workforce about what is important.

Saying 'thank you.' Last but not least, each supervisor can use the daily 'thank you' to send a powerful message about what is important and why the employee's or the team's efforts made a difference. While many organizations would benefit simply from having more supervisors say 'thank you' more often, those that can get these leaders to attach meaning to their compliments will really see a significant impact. I always expected my supervisors to thank their people on a daily basis, and they were each taught how to do this in a meaningful way. In other words, instead of simply saying the words, make sure that the employee or team is clear about what is being recognized and why their efforts made a difference.

Effectively answering the "what's in it for me?" question is primarily a matter of shaping each employee's perception of compensation fairness. If they understand the value of the well-rounded compensation package, if they can see their compensation change as success is realized, and if they receive tangible and meaningful 'thank yous' from their leaders on a regular basis, they will be much more likely to support and contribute to the lean initiative. If they are kept informed about the lean successes that are being realized and the impact that success will have on their compensation, along with their work environment, in the future, this level of support should only grow.

TAKEAWAYS

- Profit-sharing, based on better results and given frequently, will build buy-in and pride.
- Employees should be regularly informed about lean successes and their impact.
- Employees should also be rewarded and thanked for their contributions.

Incentives Should Be Based On Outcomes, Not Activities

March, 2003

You don't drive lean initiatives by rewarding people for taking part in those initiatives. You drive them by rewarding people for the outcomes of those initiatives.

That is the view of Mark Graham Brown, a Manhattan Beach, Calif., management consultant with experience in performance measurement. Brown is also the author of several books, including *Winning Score: How to Design and Implement Organizational Scorecards, Keeping Score: Using the Right Metrics to Drive World-Class Performance*, and *Baldrige Award Winning Quality*.

"The main point is not to incentivize the implementation of any program — lean, TQM, balanced scorecard — but to base incentives on what those programs produce," he says.

The metric for an incentive might be financial: an increase in business or a reduction in costs. However, "it does not have to be financial, but some important outcome," Brown adds. For example, an associate could be rewarded for achieving an improvement in safety, or an increase in employee morale.

And it isn't necessary to prove an absolute causal relationship — to prove, for example, that an increase in business was solely the result of a particular employee effort. "The test of a valid measure is 'Can I make the needle move? Can I influence it?'" Brown notes.

Where Acountability Matters

The amount of the bonuses given each December to employees of the Flexible Steel Lacing Company's plant in Downers Grove, Ill., vary from year to year, depending on business conditions. Whether each employee receives the full amount of the bonus depends partly on what that worker has done to improve the company's processes.

At Flexco, as the company is known, 20 percent of each worker's bonus is tied to a program called IPI, for implemented process improvements. Each employee must implement four process improvement ideas in the course of the year; a worker will lose 5 percent of the bonus for failure to implement one of these, or 20 percent if none are implemented.

Each process improvement effort must produce cost savings — which must be calculated — but there is no minimum amount of savings required.

There are also rewards that go with IPI efforts: A $5 gift certificate for the Subway or Blockbuster retail chains is awarded for an implementation, or the employee can request a donation to United Way. Five implementations bring a t-shirt, 10 bring a $100 gift card, and 10 per year for 4 years in a row produce a check for $400.

Flexco, which makes mechanical fastener systems for conveyor belts, has been involved in continuous improvement efforts for at least eight years, according to Bob Hafey, director of manufacturing. And the company strives to have its employees drive those efforts — which Hafey says produced $1.2 million in documented cost savings last year — at least partly through the right kinds of incentives.

"I believe we are above the crowd when it comes to empowering employees," Hafey boasts. "Individual accountability is the key to moving things forward."

New performance review procedures are also designed to drive lean behavior. Workers are reviewed by superiors and peers, and their pay increase is linked to how they score on that review. Raises occur at different times during the year, and the frequency will vary.

The mistake many companies make, he adds, is to award incentives for activity: the number of improvement projects they conduct, the number of projects completed, or even attending training about lean.

A worker might get a raise after 10 months, or after 14. If the score is low enough, there may be no raise at all.

Objectives defined during the initial review discussed at quarterly review sessions. The reviews "are driving individuals to change, to improve themselves or the business process," says Hafey. "We've seen dramatic changes in individuals. There were some who left, when told they weren't going to get an increase."

In place for a little more than a year, the new review process has worked "wonderfully," he adds. "It sends the right message. This tool allows coaches to be very honest with their folks."

One other incentive comes through certification of employee teams. Teams are certified in four phases, and completion of each phase brings a payout to each member of the team. The total of the four payouts is about $1,000, though the payout varies with the certification.

Training is necessary, of course, for continuous improvement efforts to work, and that applies even to some aspects of incentives. Workers are trained in how to fill out forms on themselves, and in filling out evaluations of their peers, for example.

Flexco has "historically been a very paternalistic company," Hafey states. "We've always treated people well. Our wage rates are above average." In business for 96 years, Flexco has never laid off workers. The head count in Downers Grove — the company's largest manufacturing site — is about 265, down 21 from 2002 due to attrition. But while sales were down in 2002, productivity was up 6 percent as measured in sales per labor hour, Hafey notes. Flexco also has manufacturing facilities in Grand Rapids, Mich., and in the United Kingdom and Australia. Sales and distribution locations include Mexico, Germany, the U.K., South Africa, Australia and New Zealand.

Overall, Hafey believes firmly that the right incentives are essential to a lean operation.

"Link rewards to performance," he stresses. "That is the essence of it. If you don't do that, you're only fooling yourself."

The problem, he explains, is that these types of measures don't necessarily produce benefits for the company. For example, if people are rewarded for the number of projects they undertake, they may not choose the projects that produce the greatest benefit;

"they will just find whatever is easy to do," Brown states.

Better measures might be improvements in revenue, reductions in cycle time or improved capacity.

Another problem Brown says he often sees in incentive programs is that "executives are on a different system than the rest of the workforce." And often their incentives are based on purely financial metrics, which he says is less effective than a system that also includes some non-financial metrics. These might include morale, safety, customer satisfaction, and/or new product development.

Ford and Federal Express are two companies that Brown says do an excellent job of structuring incentives. "They link their incentives to a balance of financial results, human resource results and customer results," he says.

Recognizing employees for their achievements is also valuable. In fact, says Brown, "a lot of times that's more effective than compensation." However, as with incentives, the recognition should be based on accomplishments rather than activities, he adds.

He also believes that a company should provide both individual and team recognition.

"Those (systems) that are all team-based tend not to work well," Brown says. "It's recognizing that in teams, some people do more than others."

TAKEAWAYS

- Activities, such as the number of improvement projects conducted, are not a good basis for incentives.
- Employees should be rewarded for improvements in revenue, reductions in cycle time or improved capacity, for example.
- The amount of a bonus may vary according to the level of improvement achieved.

23

Satisfaction Yields Improved Results

January, 2005

Employee unhappiness may be the result of problems with business processes. And by working to improve employee satisfaction, you will also improve the processes and your company's performance.

That's what executives say they have done at The Bama Companies, a Tulsa, Okla., maker of frozen food products, primarily for restaurant and fast-food chains.

"My thought was that we would go in and address the major things hitting employee satisfaction, then we would turn the wheel again and address the revenue issues," says Monty Vanderburg, director of six sigma. "We found out that employee satisfaction issues were the revenue issues."

Through a corporate-wide six sigma program launched in 2001 (which is expanding to include application of some lean principles), Bama has not only improved employee satisfaction, but also saved millions of dollars, boosted revenues and gained market share. In addition, Bama was the 2004 winner of the Malcolm Baldrige National Quality Award in the manufacturing category.

The family-owned company operates according to a philosophy of "people helping people be successful," with an insistence that all its efforts, including relationships with business partners, embody

Satisfaction of Bama employees, shown here making hand-held pies, is a top priority at the Tulsa company.

values such as trust, sharing, learning and honesty. On top of that foundation is a firm commitment to improvement strategies, including the idea that all senior managers must acquire six sigma skills. "If you want to move up, this skill set is one you need to get there," Vanderburg says, adding that CEO Paula Marshall-Chapman is the lead champion of, and driving force behind, Bama's approach.

Eliminating Stress

One of the first six sigma projects Bama launched was a review of what it calls BOMP, its Business Opportunity Management

Process. This process is designed to capture information about customers to ensure effective development of new products.

In deciding (in late 2002) to improve BOMP, Vanderburg says, Bama was concerned about three things: lead time for development of new products; "hit rate" (meaning the number of ideas that become revenue generating products) and employee satisfaction.

"People have a great deal of desire and passion around here to meet customer needs," Vanderburg boasts. "People put their own satisfaction at risk. People are working very hard and adding stress to their lives."

In seeking to address that problem, he says, Bama teams focused partly on the fact that a lot of new product ideas do not ultimately become successful products. The company has what Vanderburg says is a "very open funnel," meaning many new ideas are considered. The problem, he explains, is that employees feel "not everything I'm busting my tail on is getting to fruition, so I don't feel like I'm having an impact."

Bama's products fall primarily into three categories: hand-held pies, biscuits and pizza crust. (For example, it makes the hand-held pies sold by McDonald's.) It doesn't offer a catalog of products; new products are developed in conjunction with customers, to meet customer needs.

But in analyzing BOMP using FMEA (Failure Mode and Effects Analysis, a method of finding the root causes behind mistakes), the improvement teams found that "sometimes the customer is not fully engaged in this process," says Vanderburg. "We didn't really have a good read on the criteria. How to you tell they're committed? We were relying on phone conversations, what we hear between sales people and the customer."

New criteria were established to evaluate customer commitment. For example, one was whether the customer had an internal project person committed to the project. These new screening criteria were used to evaluate projects from 2001, and the company found that 50 percent failed the test.

The new method eliminated many less valuable ideas, but "didn't decrease the number of projects coming in the door," Vanderburg notes. "It increased our potential. Our sales force is still going to produce the opportunities, just much higher quality opportunities."

Another employee satisfaction issue the teams addressed focused on the point where products move past development and testing phases into commercialization. For employees involved in this later stage, "one of the big areas of pain is, when this project gets to me, there's not a great deal of due diligence done. Sometimes that causes stress to go back and get things done."

For example, required documentation relating to operational specifications or food safety might not have been completed.

To solve this problem, but to avoid requiring that all kinds of documentation be completed in advance on all project ideas (an unworkable approach), the improvement teams developed a list of five "drop dead" due diligence items (such as the operational specifications). For the commercialization employees, "It really gave them the power to say no, I cannot take that at this point until all these five are met. Just putting it down on paper empowered the people to say the process demands it," says Vanderburg.

Moving Forward

Bama is moving aggressively to make six sigma part of its way of operating. The effort began with eight managers being selected in 2001 for six sigma training. Today, the company says it has 13 black belts, 69 green belts and 29 yellow belts in its workforce of more than 1,000. By the end of 2005, at least 60 percent of all managers will have received training, says Vanderburg.

Lean is also becoming part of the picture. The improvement focus began with six sigma in January 2001, but "many of our projects since then have been what we now understand to be lean projects," he admits. One black belt has been designated to receive lean training and become a trainer for others within the company, leading to lean initiatives this year. Vanderburg comments, "we will take lean up a notch in 2005."

Since the six sigma initiatives began, Bama has achieved more than $11 million in savings, he states. Sales revenue has increased 47 percent since 1999.

But Vanderburg adds that financial results are only one of several measures Bama uses to gauge success. Employee satisfaction is another, of course, as are innovation and customer satisfaction.

Vanderburg also comments that there is no surprise in the key to success of Bama's initiatives: "You read this in every article, in every book, but I cannot stress enough how real this is. It has to start with the leadership of your company, and it has to be deeply rooted in the leadership or you will not succeed. If our CEO didn't believe in it 100 percent, it would have died within two years."

He notes that those Bama executives becoming black belts receive four weeks of training from a company called Smarter Solutions, with classmates from other companies. He comments, "you get to understand a little bit about the other companies, the other people, and without fail you can sit in the classroom during the first week and identify those who are going to succeed, those who have a chance and those who will fail. It's strictly by how their company is supporting six sigma."

TAKEAWAYS

- Employee satisfaction issues are often identical with business issues.
- A structured methodology is necessary to identify root causes.
- Improvement efforts will fail without top-level support.

24

Integrate Your Improvement Methods If You Want Your Initiatives to Last

September, 2004

To sustain an improvement effort so it doesn't fade after the initial burst of enthusiasm, you have to integrate it into all aspects of your business. The improvement concepts and methodology have to be an essential part of all processes and objectives.

Since 2003, Marise Clermont has been working to achieve that integration at McKesson Canada, the largest pharmaceutical distributor in that country and a provider of information products and services. As director of six sigma, she has been involved in restructuring the company's six sigma program, including changing project focus and selection, increasing management and workforce involvement, creating new objectives, and — perhaps most important — changing the way people think.

"There was a perception that six sigma is there only to improve operations and not the head office or sales or procurement or HR," she says. "Six sigma was seen as a way to resolve problems, not to improve business processes."

Since the company began implementing six sigma in 2000, there have been positive results, Clermont says, including a good return on investment, significant reduction in the level of defects for key operation indicators, and new skills and career paths for certain individuals.

But at the same time, what Clermont saw when she joined the company in 2003 was that only 1 percent of employees were actively involved with six sigma, only 10 percent of the trained green belts were doing some form of six sigma work, there was very limited implementation at the company's service center (head-quarters) and in sales, and benefits seemed to have reached a plateau.

"We began last year to have difficulty, even to have savings," she recalls. "Savings were going down a bit. We seem to be in a much better position now."

That change in position is occurring early in implementation of the new approach. It was only in March of 2004 that Clermont presented her proposals to top executives of the company, a sub-sidiary of McKesson Corporation.

Internal Integration

McKesson Canada employs 1,900 people at 15 distribution centers and operates under long-term supply agreements with retail and institutional groups. The company delivers daily to 6,000 retail pharmacies (more than 82 percent of all retail pharmacies) and 1,200 hospital pharmacies (94 percent). On top of this, McKesson offers third party logistics, in-patient and out-patient automation, software services & solutions as well as telephony and algorithm-based products and services. It is investing in automated robots and describes itself as a "significant player" in retail automation.

The Re-Alignment Plan, as it was called, serves an overall vision of making McKesson Canada a six sigma company, meaning inte-grating the tools and methodology into all areas of management, making all decisions based on facts and data, and designing and improving all business processes based on the methodology. The plan involves making changes to the company's approach to six sigma in a variety of areas, including:

A Dedicated Parent

McKesson Canada is a wholly-owned subsidiary of McKesson Corporation, a major provider of supply, information and health care management products in North America. The parent company is also an organization dedicated to Six Sigma concepts and methodology.

"We're using Six Sigma, a set of principles and methodologies used to design business practices that enhance performance by improving processes," John Hammergren, chairman and CEO, says on the company's website. "It will improve quality for our customers and fundamentally change the way we do business."

The company describes its focus as "ensuring that customers get the right drug in the right place at the right time and to assist in creating more effective supply chain processes."

McKesson, ranked 16th on the Fortune 500, has a total of 22,000 employees and, it claims, 30 percent of the North American market share for supply management in health care.

For the quarter ending June 30 of this year, McKesson reported revenues of $19.2 billion, up 16 percent from the same quarter a year earlier, and net income of $163.6 million, up 5 percent. The company also reported that Canadian revenues were up 20 percent, and Canadian operating margins improved "as a result of internal efficiencies and the customers' expanded use of a total McKesson solution."

- **Performance Evaluation.** Specific objectives were established for vice presidents for improving processes in alignment with strategic initiatives, and additional objectives were cascaded down to management, black belts and green belts. "If we don't put it in our objectives, it's difficult to realize it," Clermont comments.

- **Project Focus and Selection.** The new approach involves less emphasis on solving problems or reducing costs, with a greater focus on process improvement or design. In addition, projects have to be aligned with strategic plans.

- **Management Involvement. Six sigma** updates at executive and other meetings, and periodic project reviews by champions and process owners with black and green belts are designed to increase involvement.

- **Workforce Involvement.** New standard procedures are established to improve and design processes with facilitation tools, and black belts are coached on the new procedures. Representatives of different departments now have time commitments for sessions to work on processes. Involvement is also encouraged through kaizen events and other lean activities.

On that last point, Clermont says lean methodologies sometimes work better than six sigma approaches to get people involved. "Sometimes it's not always efficient to put a black belt on a problem," she states, adding that, with six sigma methodologies, "it can be very difficult to get buy-in, as opposed to doing something like a kaizen, or merging six sigma and lean and doing a greater team approach."

- Green Belt Program. six sigma work is now a required part of a green belt's job. Green belt projects are being aligned with strategy, and objectives now include conducting a minimum of one project per year or providing significant support to black belt projects.

- Six Sigma Program Structure. One change, Clermont notes, was to "'officialize' a dotted line between the six sigma director and the black belts.

It was there, but not strong enough."

There is also a new role for the master black belt, with a stronger focus on Canada, rather than reporting primarily to operations in the United States. And new six sigma champions are being identified for specific areas of operations.

Having several champions is important, Clermont contends, because "one person cannot do it all. Even if it's a small company, you need to have several people who are thinking of six sigma."

The overall goal, she says, is to have "a positive slope in savings."

For others involved in six sigma efforts, Clermont advises, "never do massive training of everybody without having a plan. It's better to begin small, then build slowly, rather than training everybody and creating expectations and not being able to respond to those expectations. Then the employee will say it's another flavor of the month."

TAKEAWAYS

- Sustaining improvement efforts includes finding ways to integrate them into operations.
- Performance objectives and program structure are important.
- Selecting the right projects is also essential.

Citations

(All articles taken from the *Lean Manufacturing Advisor*)

Chapter 1: "Aggressive Management Builds a New Hartz Mountain Culture." July 2003: Volume 5, Number 2

Chapter 2: "The Way[s]? to Win Hearts and Minds." July 2002 – online: Volume 4, Number 2

Chapter 3: "Creating a New Culture Is Company's First Priority." May 2003 – online: Volume 4, Number 12

Chapter 4: "Tips for Molding a Kaizen Culture." February 2000: Volume 1, Number 9

Chapter 5: "Employees Offer Suggestions When a Process Is in Place." June 2003: Volume 5, Number 1

Chapter 6: "Approach Is Key in Attempt to Make Union a Partner." November 2003: Volume 5, Number 6

Chapter 7: "The Really Tough Part: Selling Lean to the CEO." January 2004: Volume 5, Number 8

Chapter 8: "'Semi-Stealth' Strategy Turns Top Executives Into Believers." December 2004: Volume 6, Number 7

Chapter 9: "Plan to Increase Your Skills Inventory." September 2003: Volume 5, Number 4

Chapter 10: "Acquiring and Building Expertise." June 2004: Volume 6, Number 1

Chapter 11: "Plan Your Search Carefully to Get the Right Lean Leader." December 2004 – online: Volume 6, Number 7

Chapter 12: "Improving Hiring Processes Saves Both Time and Money." December 2003 – online: Volume 5, Number 7

Chapter 13: "Ten Critical Areas Where Supervisors Need Your Help With Culture Change." July 2001: Volume 3, Number 2

Chapter 14: "Structured Program Builds Skills of Team Leaders." December 2003: Volume 5, Number 7

Chapter 15: "Want a High-Level Job Here? You Better Learn Lean First." July 2004: Volume 6, Number 2

Chapter 16: "Plastic Firm's Lean Team Is Its Source of New Talent." November 2002: Volume 4, Number 6

Chapter 17: "An Assessment Tool Tells You Whether Your Culture Is Lean." October 2004: Volume 6, Number 5

Chapter 18: "Nine Steps for Getting TPM Buy-In From Varied Groups." December 1999: Volume 1, Number 7

Chapter 19: "Frequent Feedback Fosters Change[s] in Company Culture." February 2004: Volume 5, Number 9

Chapter 20: "A Good Day of Production Begins With a Good Meeting." January 2005 – online: Volume 6, Number 8

Chapter 21: "Compensation Helps Lean Pay Off." December 2004: Volume 6, Number 7

Chapter 22: "Incentives Should Be Based on Outcomes, Not Activities." March 2003: Volume 4, Number 10

Chapter 23: "Satisfaction Yields Improved Results." January 2005: Volume 6, Number 8

Chapter 24: "Integrate [Your] Improvement Methods if You Want [Your] Initiatives to Last." September 2004: Volume 6, Number 4

Index

Lean Manufacturing Advisor ...

Your Monthly, Independent Source for First-Hand, Current, and Practical Advice.

If the articles in this book are proving helpful, and you want to stay current on the latest trends and developments in lean implementation, then you should subscribe to *Lean Manufacturing Advisor.*

Lean Manufacturing Advisor's editorial team gives you the behind-the-scenes news and advice, and real-life, how-to-implement details from people on the same continuous improvement journey as you. Its in-depth coverage demonstrates how you can be an effective agent of change and lead management and front line employees in a successful lean transformation.

Each month *Lean Manufacturing Advisor* covers the latest developments in lean manufacturing with these unique features:

- Case studies, featuring successful real-life lean initiatives, provide a wealth of ideas to share with your team.

- The Q&A section addresses common technical questions.

- Editorials offer advice, analysis, and commentary on the latest developments in lean manufacturing.

- Photos, diagrams, and samples documents show you what other companies are doing.

When you subscribe to *Lean Manufacturing Advisor,* you join a community of experienced executives and managers who have successfully implemented lean in their organizations. You'll leverage their experience, benchmark your progress, avoid the pitfalls, and speed lean implementation.

Get the insider's view that you can't find on corporate websites or in trade magazines, subscribe to *Lean Manufacturing Advisor!*

To subscribe, visit our website: www.productivitypress.com, or call toll-free at 1-888-319-5852. For multiple subscriptions of 3 or more copies, contact us at ehanus@productivitypress.com.